DATE DUE		
JUN 0 8 1993 APR 1 4 2000		
JUN 1 5 1993 APR 1 7 2000		
FEB 2 8 1994 AUG 2 3 2001		
MAR 2 9 1994		
APR 2 1 1994		
MAY 2 1 1996		
MAR 1 7 2000 MAR 3 0 2000		
APR 1 0 2000 4/12/2001		

Canadian Fiction Studies

Other volumes in preparation

Introducing
MARGARET ATWOOD'S

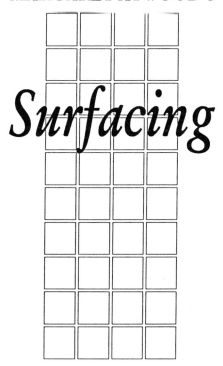

Surfacing

A READER'S GUIDE BY
George Woodcock

ECW PRESS

CANADIAN CATALOGUING IN PUBLICATION DATA

Woodcock, George, 1912–
Introducing Margaret Atwood's Surfacing

(Canadian fiction studies ; no. 4)
Bibliography : p. 70.
Includes index.
ISBN 1–55022–020–9

I. Atwood, Margaret, 1939– . Surfacing.
I. Title. II. Series.

PS8501.T86S878 1990   C813′.54   C89–094999–9
PR9199.3.A87S878 1990

This book has been published with the assistance of grants
from The Canada Council, the Ontario Arts Council, and
the Government of Canada Department of Communications.

The cover features a reproduction of the dust-wrapper
of the first edition of *Surfacing*, courtesy of the
Thomas Fisher Rare Book Library, University of Toronto.
Frontispiece photograph courtesy Graeme Gibson © 1990,
reproduced courtesy of the photographer.
Design and imaging by ECW Type & Art, Oakville, Ontario.
Printed by University of Toronto Press, North York, Ontario.

Distributed by Butterworths Canada Ltd.
75 Clegg Road, Markham, Ontario L6G IAI

Published by ECW PRESS,
307 Coxwell Avenue, Toronto, Ontario M4L 3B5

Table of Contents

A Note on the Author

Born in Winnipeg in 1912, George Woodcock went to England in his infancy, and remained there until he returned in 1949 to Canada, on whose Pacific coast he has lived ever since. In the late 1930s he began to publish his poetry in magazines like *New Verse* and *Twentieth Century Verse* and moved into English literary circles where his friends included George Orwell, Kathleen Raine, Dylan Thomas, Herbert Read, and Julian Symons. He founded *Now*, a radical literary magazine which he ran from 1940 to 1947, acted for a period as joint editor of another journal, *Freedom*, and began to establish himself in the English literary world with his books of poetry and with prose works like *William Godwin: A Biography* (1946) and *The Paradox of Oscar Wilde* (1950). Since returning to Canada he has travelled in Asia, the Americas, the South Pacific, and Europe, and has produced many travel books. Most recently he has been to northern China, where he travelled up the Silk Road and into the Gobi Desert, describing his journey in *The Caves in the Desert* (1988). He has also published more verse; a number of important critical works, including *The Crystal Spirit: A Study of George Orwell* (1966), *Dawn and the Darkest Hour: A Study of Aldous Huxley* (1972), and *Thomas Merton: Monk and Poet* (1978); and a number of historical works including *The British in the Far East* (1969), *Who Killed the British Empire: An Inquest* (1974), *The Social History of Canada* (1988), and *The Marvelous Century* (1988), an account of the 6th century BC.

His writing on Canada has been considerable. He founded the critical journal, *Canadian Literature*, has written a history of the Doukhobors and biographies of Gabriel Dumont and Amor de Cosmos; and critical studies of Hugh MacLennan, Mordecai Richler, Matt Cohen, Patrick Lane, and Charles Heavysege. Three volumes of his critical essays have been published: *Odysseus Ever Returning: Essays on Canadian Writers and Writings* (1970), *The World of Canadian Writing: Critiques and Recollections* (1980), and *Northern Spring: The Flowering of Canadian Literature* (1987). The first volume of his auto-biography (*Letter to the Past*) appeared in 1982, and the second, *Beyond the Blue Mountain*, in 1987. He has won the Molson Prize of The Canada Council, the Governor-General's Award for non-fiction, the University of British Columbia Medal for Popular Biography (twice), and the National Magazines Award (three times).

Introducing
Margaret Atwood's
Surfacing

Chronology

1939   Margaret Eleanor Atwood born in Ottawa, 18 November.

1945   Her family moves to Sault Ste. Marie and the following year to Toronto, spending so much time in the northern bush where her father works as a forest entomologist in Québec that Atwood does not "attend a full year of school until . . . grade eight."

1955   Begins writing.

1961   Publishes her first volume of verse, *Double Persephone*, which wins E.J. Pratt Medal. Graduates with B.A. from Victoria College, Toronto, and leaves for Harvard with a Woodrow Wilson Fellowship.

1963–65   Works for a Canadian market research company and writes a yet unpublished novel.

1965   Teaches English at the University of British Columbia and writes *The Edible Woman*.

1966   Her book of poems, *The Circle Game*, is published and wins the Governor-General's Award.

1967   Marries James Polk.

1967–68   Teaches at Sir George Williams University, Montreal.

1968   *The Edible Woman* (novel) and *The Animals in That Country* (verse) published, the latter having won first prize in Centennial Poetry Competition, 1967.

1969–70   Teaches at the University of Alberta.

1970   *Procedures from Underground* and *Journals of Susanna Moodie* (both verse).

1971	*Power Politics* (verse).
1971–72	Teaches at York University, Toronto.
1971–73	Associated as editor with the House of Anansi Press.
1972	*Surfacing* (novel) and *Survival: A Thematic Guide to Canadian Literature.*
1972–73	Writer-in-residence, University of Toronto.
1973	Divorce from James Polk. Moves to a farm near Alliston, Ont., with Graeme Gibson, novelist.
1974	*You Are Happy* (verse) which wins Bess Hopkins Prize from *Poetry* (Chicago). Receives honorary LL.D. from Queen's University.
1976	*Selected Poems* and *Lady Oracle* (novel), which wins City of Toronto Book Award. Her daughter, Eleanor Jess Atwood Gibson, born.
1977	*Days of the Rebels,* 1815–40 (history) and *Dancing Girls* (short stories), which wins St. Lawrence Medal for Fiction and Award for Short Fiction of Periodical Distributors of Canada. *Lady Oracle* wins Canadian Booksellers Association award.
1978	*Two-Headed Poems* and *Up in a Tree* (children's fiction).
1979	*Life before Man* (novel).
1980	*Anna's Pet* (children's fiction). Moves to Toronto and becomes vice-president of Writers-Union of Canada, of which she is president in 1981. Receives Graduate Society Medal from Radcliffe College, Harvard, and Honorary Litt.D., from Concordia University.
1981	*Bodily Harm* (novel) and *True Stories* (verse). Awarded Molson Prize.
1982	*Second Words: Collected Critical Prose.* Edits the *New Oxford Book of Canadian Verse in English.* Wins Welsh Arts Council International Writers' Prize.
1983	*Murder in the Dark: Short Fictions and Prose Poems* and

Bluebird's Egg (short stories).
Honorary D. Litt., University of Toronto.
Interlunar (poems).

1984–86   President of P.E.N. International Canadian Branch.

1985   *The Handmaid's Tale* (fiction) which receives Governor-General's Award and *Los Angeles Times* Prize and is runner up for Booker Prize.

1986   *Selected Poems II: Poems New and Selected 1976–86.*
Collaborates with Robert Weaver in editing *The Oxford Book of Canadian Short Stories in English.*
Receives Toronto Arts Award and Ida Nudel Humanitarian Award of Canadian Jewish Congress.

1987   Receives American Humanist of the Year Award.

1988   *Cat's Eye* (novel).

The Importance of the Work

1972, which was Margaret Atwood's own thirty-third year, may have been the most important of her literary career, for it was then that she began to reveal the full potentialities of her creativity.

She was already known as one of the best of the younger Canadian poets, with six volumes already to her credit, of which *The Circle Game* had won the Governor-General's Award in 1966. She was working currently on the terse, elliptical poems of *Power Politics* (1973), in which she would deal once again with the dark aspects of relationships between women and men and the broader human discordances with the natural environment, both of which modern people are in her view fatally inclined to gloss over with self-reassuring myths of order and progress.

If Atwood prepared but did not publish a book of verse in 1972, she did bring out in that year the two books which broadened her public image from that of a rapidly developing young poet into that of an accomplished and influential woman-of-letters.

The first of these was *Survival*, important in the context of Canadian writing (present and past) as the presentation of our literary history in terms of traditions of fiction and verse that give expression to strong collective fears regarding our survival as a distinct Canadian culture.

Even more than a work of literary criticism, in which role it often seemed to be marred by hasty generalization, *Survival* was important as a tract against cultural colonialism. For Atwood it was a first declaration of the Canadian nationalism that has remained an important factor in her attitudes as a public personality, and equally, since Atwood does not believe that in our age a writer can be other than actively engaged as soon as he sets his hand to pencil, in her writing and particularly in the more public genre of fiction.

Survival describes itself as "A Thematic Guide to Canadian Literature," and here it reveals what at first sight may seem a fundamental discrepancy in Atwood's attitudes towards the various literary genres, for, while in her verse she tends to be formally austere and philosophically tortuous, in her fiction she is inclined to be didactic — unashamed to be teaching a lesson — and satiric in the classic sense of commanding reformation by laughter.

It will be evident that the novel which would fulfil the demands of a thematic attitude of the kind outlined in *Survival* cannot be avant-gardist in the sense of proving the autonomous nature of art by conducting experiments detached from actual or at least probable existence. For Atwood art is a re-exploration of life with a view to bringing men and women closer to an understanding of the evil — and occasionally the good — that characterized their true relation with each other and with the natural world. She is an intensely moral writer, and even if she has written nothing so openly propagandist as Hugh MacLennan's early nationalist novels, *Barometer Rising* and *Two Solitudes*, an argument is always being worked out in her novels, usually obliquely and always in terms of human experience.

For very similar reasons the kind of novel that Margaret Atwood writes develops its own kind of realism; realism has always been the dominant mode in Canadian fiction, each novelist modifying it according to his needs. When she wishes to be satirical for example, Atwood tends towards the rearrangement of plausibilities rather than towards comic fantasy; given the basic situation of the novel, the characters could consistently act as they do, though the result of such consistency may be ludicrous. Where Atwood does use fantasy — as we shall see when we examine *Surfacing* more closely — it is a product of the protagonist's abnormal state of mind, consistent in its own terms, so that we have a convincing hallucinatory world developing parallel to the equally convincing world of actuality in which the characters find themselves, and the result is at times rather like the disturbing effect of those surrealist paintings where all the details are rendered with naturalist accuracy yet another kind of intelligence has arranged them.

Surfacing is a novel whose importance lies in its role as the first successful novel of a writer who already, even before its appearance, seemed destined to become a leader of the generation of young and talented writers emerging during the early 1970s. As in the case of its predecessor, *The Edible Woman* (Atwood's first novel, published in 1969), its preoccupations seem to derive less from the influence of identifiable novelists than from the long series of meditations on the falsities of human perceptions in the modern age which she developed independently in her poetry. But the relationship within her oeuvre, between the first and second novel, *is* close enough to see in *Surfacing* the establishment of a thematic and a structural pattern that continues through Atwood's novels down to the present. They are really novels of individuation, and the presence of C.G. Jung, far more subtly integrated than he is in the clumsy and obvious novels of Robertson Davies, seems never far distant.

Always the propagandist is a woman, and always the woman is young but old enough for her experience of the modern world to have driven her into some kind of life crisis. There are no old women — no Hagar Shipleys — among Atwood's heroines, nor, except in the recollection of past experience, is any of her leading characters a young girl.

They are all in fact women who have accepted the morës of the twentieth-century consumer society and lived according to them, in many cases by directly serving that society. Marian McAlpin, in *The Edible Woman*, is actually a consumer research analyst (as Margaret Atwood herself was for a period). The unnamed narrator and protagonist of *Surfacing* is a commercial artist. Rennie Wilford in *Bodily Harm* (probably the best of Atwood's novels after *Surfacing*) is what she calls a "life-styles journalist," making her living by writing on food and fashion in a way that implies a support of the consumer-oriented society and an acceptance of its values. External circumstances or inner compulsions break the easy accommodations they seem to have made with their world. They are released, by mental breakdown or by political accident, to the darker forces within themselves or in the world outside, to the latter of which they respond in ambivalent ways. Out of such responses there emerges a symbolic pattern of self-recreation resembling, as we shall see in considering *Surfacing*, a traditional initiation.

The result, which characterizes Atwood's fiction as a whole and which made her early novels seem so remarkable at the time of publication, was what one might call an anti-social realism. Social realism assumes the presence and necessity of a given social order within which the characters interact. Even novelists with a politically revolutionary intent tend to proceed from the assumption that what is wrong with any modern society can be righted by progress achieved through a more rational and scientific ordering of society which leads it further away from the apparent disorder of natural (or primitive) living. Atwood proceeds from the assumption that the society which has emerged from a reliance on logic, and which defies the natural instinctual urges will be a sick one. It will produce emotionally sick people who will only be able to cure themselves by challenging and defeating its manifestations within themselves. The social novel was based on observing the interaction of human beings within a given and accepted social situation. In *Surfacing* — and before it in *The Edible Woman* — the social situation is not accepted; it is liberation through self-understanding and self-realization that the individual is led towards, and this of course produces a new attitude towards the character, who is seen from within rather than in a constantly changing dramatic relationship with others. In this pioneering rejection perhaps lies Margaret Atwood's importance as an innovatory influence in Canadian fiction, for she has had many followers.

Critical Reception

By the time Margaret Atwood published *Surfacing* in 1972 a considerable body of criticism had built up around her early books of poetry and her first novel, *The Edible Woman*. In the latter case, publication in Britain and the United States led to critical notice in those countries as well as in Canada, and already a territorial pattern that has been remarkably consistent began to emerge. In Canada, especially after *Survival*, with its polemics against cultural colonialism, it was Atwood's Canadian nationalism that tended to draw attention from the aesthetic merits of her work, whereas to American reviewers, among whom little was known about Canadian collective passions, it seemed obvious that her main stress was on the plight of women in the modern world, and the feminist critics took her under their wing. In both countries, especially after the publication of *Surfacing*, an ecological direction began to emerge in comments on her writing, recognizing her concern over the discordance between modern materially oriented civilization and the natural world. In Britain there has been throughout a greater tendency to see her work in predominantly literary terms, outside its possible polemical intent.

It is useful at least briefly to dwell on the critical response to the early poetry, since, as I once remarked about Margaret Atwood, she is not one of those poets whose writing in prose seems separate except in formal terms from their verse. On the contrary, "the capillary links between her poetry, her fiction, her criticism, are many and evident" (McCombs 92). A phrase in a poem becomes a theme in a novel; characters sketched out in the barely differentiated personae of the poetry become full human beings in the developing process of fiction; the critical arguments in *Survival* and in the later essays on literature collected in *Second Words* (1984) often develop notions adumbrated in the early books of poetry or anticipate those which are developed in the later novels.

Atwood's first chapbook of poetry, *Double Persephone* (1961), aroused little critical attention, though it won her a Pratt Medal. But her second book, *The Circle Game*, appearing five years later, not only won her the Governor General's Award, but aroused the attention — and usually the admiration — of the critics, some of the most interesting and perceptive of whom were Atwood's fellow poets.

Michael Ondaatje, for example, is already sketching out in his *Canadian Forum* (April 1967) review the world of the mind that *Surfacing* will share with the early poems. Comparing Margaret Atwood's early poems with Gwen MacEwen's, he remarks that:

> Unlike Gwen MacEwen, Margaret Atwood does not need to make forays, now and then, into the world of mythology, for her book is full of her own personal mythologies. The people she creates, or the poses she assumes for herself, are aspects of a well-rounded fully realised imaginative world. (McCombs 29)

In Atwood's poems, Ondaatje suggests, "private and traditional worlds blend into one," myth is "given such immediacy and humanity that we scarcely recognize it," and the worlds the poet presents "have the form and violence of mythologies but none of the expected grandeur and costumes." Opposed to this poet's world of "monstrous battles" Ondaatje sets "the ordered too-clean world which Margaret Atwood pits herself against like an arsonist, well armed with 'remnants of ancestors / fossil bones and fangs.' "

In doing so he is of course hitting on the lines of continuity between Atwood's poetry and her fiction, for this is the very world of oppositions one encounters in *The Edible Woman* and *Surfacing*, while Ondaatje also anticipates the anthropophagy that is central to the plot and the theme of *The Edible Woman* when he talks of the poetic persona evoked in *The Circle Game* as "the cannibalistic speaker who demands to know everything of the people around her" (McCombs 30).

None of the reviewers of Atwood's early books of poetry anticipated quite as accurately and fully as Ondaatje the resemblances that later would occur between them and the early novels, though Robin Skelton isolated an element strongly present in *Surfacing* when reviewing Atwood's two 1970 collections (*The Journals of Susanna*

Moodie and *Procedures for Underground*) in the *Malahat Review* (January 1971), where he detects in them "a certain gothic enjoyment of the unnameable terror and the hallucinations of solitude" (Mc-Combs 34).

Later, in reviewing *The Edible Woman* on its first appearance and in various writings on Atwood that were incorporated in my 1975 essay on her in the anthology, *The Canadian Novel in the Twentieth Century*, I myself stressed the strikingly close links between her verse and her novels.

Indeed, the identity between the poems and *The Edible Woman* is so close that it was with a sense of *déjà vu* that I read *Power Politics* not long after a second reading of the novel, for both concern the cruelties of love, the Proustian impenetrability it encounters, and when I try to think of a quick way of saying what *The Edible Woman* is about, a verse from *The Circle Game* comes immediately to my mind.

These days we keep
 our weary distances:
sparring in the vacant spaces
 of peeling rooms
 and rented minutes, climbing
 all the expected stairs, our voices
 abraded with fatigue,
 our bodies weary.

The Edible Woman, too, is about the distances and defences between human beings. The distances and defences are necessary — the suggestion is not even skin deep — because human beings are predatory. *The Edible Woman* is a novel about emotional cannibalism. (McCombs 92–93)

Again, when Margaret Atwood's second novel, *Surfacing*, and her topography of the Canadian literary consciousness, *Survival*, were published almost simultaneously in the autumn of 1972 it was the striking continuities with the books of verse that impressed me. I had been struck by the way in which, in her most recent book of verse, *Power Politics*, she had developed a spare personal poetic, with poems as defensively economical as cactuses, which seemed to extend into a whole personal ethic.

> Beyond truth,
> tenacity . . . .
> . . . of this cactus, gathering
> itself together
> against the sand, yes tough
> rind & spikes but doing
> the best it can. (*Selected Poems*, 160)

And now I found this ethic and the poetic that seemed to have emerged from it, being developed in more discursive form in two prose works of undeniable importance. I found the continuity, the sense of an extraordinarily self-possessed mind at work on an integrated structure of literary architecture, not only interesting and indeed exciting so far as it concerned Margaret Atwood herself, but equally interesting and exciting as an index to the development of our literary tradition; even a decade before, it would have been impossible to think of the Canadian ambiance fostering this kind of confident and sophisticated sensibility. I expressed these views at the time, writing of both *Survival* and *Surfacing* in *Canadian Literature* at the time of publication, but since my views on *Surfacing* will take their places more elaborately in the remainder of this book, I will go on to other critical reactions to *Surfacing* at the time of its publication and later on.

It was with the publication of *Surfacing* that Margaret Atwood became regarded, perhaps more than she had bargained for, as a woman novelist speaking especially for and to women. There have always been ambivalences in her attitude towards feminism — the kind of reservations which one often encounters among writers who are reluctant to see their political and social inclinations, based on natural sympathies, constricted into the conduit of a party line.

I think Canadian writers, and particularly Canadian woman writers, have understood her position rather better than their feministically inclined American counterparts. For example, in a very early notice of *Surfacing* in *Maclean's* (1972) Christina Newman praised the book, which "moves from the plain perceptions of the opening chapters onto the knife edge of madness and fantasy that are characteristic of Atwood's vision," for its excellence in "conveying what goes on in the mind of a woman trying to deal with the little brutalities inflicted on her body and spirit by the harsh politics of sex." But she sees the real triumph of the book as, in its own way, a nationalist one: the evocation in her portrayal of the Northern wilderness of Canada as it is, as we actually experience it.

> She writes with the ease of total acceptance from right inside the culture, authenticating our experience, holding up a mirror so that the image we get back is not distorted by satire or made unreal by proselytizing, not disguised as "universal" for the export market, not aimed at the Leacock medal but real — as real, say, as the Chicago of Nelson Algren. It's this space, this place, an answer to the famous Northrop Frye question, Where Is Here? Here is where we've been and when we go again it'll be different, clearer because Atwood's written about it. (McCombs 44)

Margaret Laurence, writing in *Quarry* (Spring 1973), implicitly recognised her successor as Canada's leading novelist by describing *Surfacing* as "a novel so striking that I become evangelical about it" (McCombs 45). For Laurence, the novel had many themes, but most important among them was the ecological, which she found expressed in Atwood's search for the meaning of a human life shadowed always by morality.

> The themes are many, and the nature of reality is one of the most interesting. Some of the themes concern our most burning contemporary issues — the role of women, the facts of urban life, and most of all, the wounding and perhaps killing of our only home, Earth. Margaret Atwood is one of the very few novelists writing today who can deal with these issues without ever writing propaganda. Perhaps she has been able to do this partly because she has interwoven all these themes with the theme which is central to our mythology, our religions, our history and (whether we know it or not) our hearts — humankind's quest for the archetypal parents, for our gods, and for our own meanings in the face of our knowledge of the inevitability of death. (McCombs 47)

Two important American pieces on Margaret Atwood appeared in 1973, Joan Larkin's review of *Surfacing* and *Power Politics* in *Ms.*, and

Marge Piercy's "Margaret Atwood: Beyond Victimhood" in the *American Poetry Review*, dealing with all of Atwood's books up to and including *Surfacing*. Larkin is cautious in the way she imposes a feminist pattern on Atwood's work. She actually quotes Atwood's denial (in the preface to an American edition of *Power Politics*) that her works were products of "what is commonly termed the Women's Movement"; Atwood remarks that "parallel lines do not usually start from the same point, and . . . being adopted is not, finally, the same as being born" (McCombs 52).

More impetuously, Marge Piercy insists that all the qualifications for adoption being met, Atwood should acknowledge her allegiance to "a woman's culture" (McCombs 53).

> With her concern with living by eating, with that quest for the self that Barbara Demming has found at the heart of major works by women from the past 150 years (*Liberation*, Summer 1973), with her passion for becoming conscious of one's victimization and ceasing to acquiesce, with her insistence on nature as a living whole of which we are all interdependent parts, with her respect for the irrational center of the psyche and the healing experiences beyond logical control, her insistence on joining the divided head and body, her awareness of roleplaying and how women suffocate in the narrow crevices of sexual identity, she is part of that growing women's culture already, a great quilt for which we are each stitching our own particolored blocks out of old petticoats, skirts, coats, bedsheets, blood, and berry juice. (McCombs 66)

Perhaps the most interesting feature of these early American notices is one to which I shall return in discussing the novel itself in greater detail, Joan Larkin's suggestion that the "voyage of discovery" of the protagonist in *Surfacing*, her "madness," is "much like the trip into inner space and time that R.D. Laing described in *The Politics of Experience* as a natural healing process" (McCombs 50).

Very soon, as Atwood's repute increased during the 1970s, the various studies of her work in general and of *Surfacing* in particular became steadily more numerous, so that it is impossible here to discuss or even mention all of them. Four good selections of Atwood criticism have appeared, and various views of the novel can be traced by reading them. They are: *Margaret Atwood: A Symposium* (a special issue of *Malahat Review*), edited by Linda Sandler (1977); *The Art of Margaret Atwood: Essays in Criticism*, edited by Arnold E. Davidson and Cathy N. Davidson (1981); *Margaret Atwood: Language, Text and System*, edited by Sherill E. Grace and Lorraine Weir (1983); and *Critical Essays on Margaret Atwood*, edited by Judith McCombs (1988). Surprisingly, considering the broad international interest that exists in Atwood, no critic has yet published a major study of her work. Two of the books in existence are Jerome H. Rosenberg's *Margaret Atwood* (1984), which shares the shallowness one expects of the Twayne's World Author Series in which it appeared, and Frank Davey's highly polemical *Margaret Atwood: A Feminist Poetics* (1984). Neither offers us much in the way of new insights.

However, Atwood has inevitably attracted the attention of the dominant critics who tend to shape the course of our understanding of Canadian literature and its development, and it is worth glancing at their views of *Surfacing* to gain some idea of the changing critical standing of the novel.

Only two years after *Surfacing* was published, Frank Davey included it in his survey of English-Canadian literature since 1960, *From There to Here* (1974). His attitude, as in his later book on Atwood, is sharply critical. He treats *The Edible Woman* and *Surfacing* together, stressing their resemblances and the fact that, as in her earlier poems, "the two central issues are man's attitude to an unstable and treacherous universe and man's tendency to apply his manipulative and exploitive treatment of that universe to his fellow man" (33).

Having established his view of the essentially didactic nature of Atwood's fiction, Davey goes on:

> These two books show Atwood to be a novelist brilliant at the verbal level of dialogue and epigram but methodical in her handling of characterization and structure. Both novels have the same narrative pattern: a young woman of growing manipulativeness and cynicism finds that her body is rebelling and alienating her from the rationalist friends who have been killing her spirit; this rebellion ultimately saves her. Both novels have the same cast of characters: a sensitive young woman with a high potential for body rebellion plus variously grasping minor

characters who have sold their souls to fashion and consumerism. Both works are clearly "thesis novels" in which depth of characterization and credibility of action have been sacrificed to make vividly clear the danger and profound unnaturalness of disembodied rationalism and human exploitation. (34)

The second edition of the *Literary History of Canada* appeared in 1976, and in his section on the fiction published since 1960 W.H. New included Atwood's first two novels, declaring *Surfacing* much the better book and noting that it "declares the author's intentional laconic totality, her affirmation of people as extensions of their landscape, and her conviction that compassion can be an excuse for reluctance to become politically engaged" (III, 273). He notes how the victim, the central metaphor of *Survival*, "appears very strongly in *Surfacing* as the link between the femaleness of the central character and the dilemma of the nation in which she lives." Drawing nearer to the heart of the novel, he remarks:

Paramount in *Surfacing* is a sense of evil, and the book, locating it in Americanisms, imbalances, and losses of identity, probes its way towards a knowledge of when and how it began. The horn and garden imagery in the book takes on significant moral dimensions, and the quest for knowledge itself — which had been the impulse behind Canadian historical expansion — is seen as an ambivalent pursuit. That resolution does not deter the author from her nationalist fervour; it does, however, make her pro-Canadianism more than empty chauvinism and give it a complex ethical cast. (274)

Five years later, by 1981, when John Moss published his survey of major Canadian fiction, *A Reader's Guide to the Canadian Novel*, *Surfacing* had moved into an almost classic position in the canon of Canadian writing, and was being appreciated less for its themes than for the formal skills Atwood had carried on from her poetry and adapted to prose fiction. Moss, who described it as "a formidable achievement, brilliantly accomplished," values it in these terms, as an extraordinary merging of perception and verbal achievement.

Atwood has a perfect command of images and words as poetic determinants of reality. That is, image and word not only describe something, they become that something, as it is perceived

or conceived. Thus, the *idea* of a fish jumping is the reality . . . .
The word "tree" joins speaker to object; they become one.
Atwood offers us the reality her narrator perceives/conceives,
and appearance and reality merge. (14)

Shortly afterwards (1983), writing on Atwood in the *Oxford Companion to Canadian Literature*, Rosemary Sullivan interpreted the
retreat of the heroine of *Surfacing* into the wilderness, "which is both
a literal and a psychological place," as Atwood's challenge to "Western ways of seeing, particularly of relating to nature."

The modern compulsion is to treat nature as raw material, to
explain and master it in accordance with the technological myth
of progress. By showing her protagonist moving through a ritual
preparation that corresponds to the stages of shamanistic initiation, Atwood attempts to recover a primitive, mystical participation in nature, in which the heroine must recreate herself. (32)

Three years later, in the 1986 edition of the English compilation,
Contemporary Novelists, George Woodcock examined Margaret
Atwood's work in an international context, declaring her to be "one
of Canada's most versatile writers" (49). He described *Surfacing* as
the account of a *rite de passage*: "it is a novel of self-realization, hence
of life-realization," in which "surfacing" becomes possible "only
after submersion," as is emphasized by the recurrence of metaphors
involving drowning.

Her [the narrator's] brother is almost drowned as a child; her
father, she discovers, drowned searching for Indian paintings on
a rock wall falling sheer to the lake; her own crisis is precipitated
when, diving to locate the paintings, she encounters her father's
floating corpse; her surfacing becomes almost literally a rising
from death into life. (50)

But it is a surfacing that in the end represents a journey through
and beyond the "primitive, mystical participation in nature" of which
Sullivan wrote.

"I" must shed all she had acquired, unlearn adulthood, return
through childhood, and become like the victim animals, as she
is when, fleeing from her companions and living like a beast, she
returns to a consciousness beyond the animistic. The gods have

departed; she is alone: "The lake is quiet, the trees surround me, asking and giving nothing."

One senses, as the novel ends, that benign indifference of the universe of which Camus spoke.

Woodcock warned readers that *Surfacing* "also contains a strong element of self-mockery" (50).

Shortly beforehand, in his *Canadian Literature in English*, published late in 1985, W.J. Keith had reinforced Woodcock's idea of the self-mockery present in *Surfacing*, by stressing its multiple ironies and ambiguities.

> The loss of individuality is here rendered ironically by the employment of a narrator whose character we come to know intimately but whose name we never discover. A novel about lying, madness, guilt, and the elusiveness of the past, it is also tantalizingly ambiguous. Within it a Swiftian trap is set against superficial present-day assumptions: the lies and madness belong as much to the generation of the late 1960s as to the society against which they rebelled; the deep-rooted psychological guilt emerges as the result of an abortion; the past can only be re-entered by giving up not merely what makes us modern but what makes us human.... If on one level it is a quest for identity, on another it virtually parodies the possibility of such a quest. (163)

Perhaps the leading ambiguity that various critics have noticed in *Surfacing* lies in the fact that though Atwood speaks consciously and selectively of the myths by which we live, and stresses the need to recognize them, she also stresses the need to work our way through them into the real world where we are condemned to dwell. In a long essay exploring Atwood's fiction in *Canadian Writers and Their Works* (Fiction Series, Volume Nine) Ildikó de Papp Carrington concluded her lengthy 1987 study of Atwood's fiction by remarking of the narrator that, after all,

> she cannot become a tree or part of the earth: she is a human being forced to abandon the mythical world of the romance and to live in the real one, unsatisfactory though it may be. (65)

Reading of the Text

THE THUMB MARKS OF THE MAKER

More than any other of Margaret Atwood's novels, with the possible exception of *Bodily Harm*, *Surfacing* strikes one as a work of consummate virtuosity; the limpid style and the apparently simple plot of this comparatively short novel in fact embrace a great variety of themes, a multitude of literary echoes, and more questions than answers. It is obviously the product of a mind remarkable for its balancing elements of intellect and intuition, "an unusual combination," as Marge Piercy has called it, "of wit and satiric edge, a fine critical intelligence, and an ability to go deep into the irrational earth of the psyche" (McCombs 53). It is a mind that has produced a poetry of remarkable verbal precision and emotional evocativeness, as well as some of the best of recent criticism (written in the interstices of a busy creative life) and that finds nothing human beyond its interest and sympathy, with human including by extension the rest of the earthly community of living beings in which men and women live on the earth.

The experience and knowledge Atwood had avidly gathered (she was only thirty-three when *Surfacing* was published) are clearly evident in the novel, leaving their traces like the thumb marks of a potter. There is her childhood in the Canadian northland that provides the setting in which *Surfacing* is enacted. There is the naturalist's power of observing and describing that she acquired from her entomologist father and her childhood reading of the great French insect man Henri Fabre and the other marvellous naturalist writers of the nineteenth century. The academic studies on the grotesque in literature which she followed at Harvard leave their mark in the heavy element of Gothicism and ghost story that contribute to the climax in *Surfacing*. The awareness of a nation's alienation that prompted her to write *Survival* as a result of her readings in Canadian literature permeates the novel, but it is rendered ironically — in the tone of self-mockery I have already mentioned. The same could be said of the way she brings in the concerns that troubled her and other Canadian writers at the beginning of the 1970s — the position and role of women in society, the aspects of colonialism and particularly the way American intrusions have shaped our attitudes as Canadians, and the difficulty of reconciling the fact of being human with the reality of what humanity has done to other creatures and to earth itself, the mother to whom it owes its existence and its increasingly problematical survival.

We have, emerging from these elements, a novel in which the recurrent didacticism of the narrative is undermined by the irony of the tone, and I suggest it may be a good beginning, before we read it in conventional terms of plot and character, of voice and time and memory, to establish the author's own attitude to fiction. What does she see as its purpose, and what does she see as the role of the novelist? And where does she see *Surfacing* in the fictional tradition?

To those who have been impressed by the extravagant imaginativeness — and at times the sheer playfulness — that at times break out in Atwood's novels, it may seem surprising that in her own statements about her own work she stresses the "descriptive" and the "moral" aspects of fiction. Authors to her are not only private people; "they are transmitters of their culture." And she sees as almost inevitable, and certainly a fact in her own case, the evolution of the writer from his early fascination with the language to his later involvement with what William Godwin (that early predecessor of Atwood who also combined social realism with Gothic fantasy) would call "Things As They Are."

Writing in her book of essays, *Second Words*, Atwood discusses her "growing involvement with human rights issues," and remarks that for her these are not "separate from writing." She continues:

When you begin to write, you deal with your immediate surroundings; as you grow, your immediate surroundings become larger. There's no contradiction.

When you begin to write you're in love with the language, with the act of creation, with yourself partly; but as you go on, the writing — if you follow it — will take you places you never intended to go and show you things you would never otherwise have seen. I began as a profoundly apolitical writer, but then I began to do what all novelists and some poets do: I began to describe the world around me. (14)

And a little farther on in the same book, in an essay written in 1980, eight years after the publication of *Surfacing*, Atwood goes on to examine the role of fiction as one of the few still active ways in which society and the interaction of people within it can be honestly scrutinized.

Especially now that organized religion is scattered and in disarray, and politicians have, Lord knows, lost their credibility, fiction is one of the few forms left through which we may examine our society not in its particular but in its typical aspects; through which we can see ourselves and the ways in which we behave towards each other, through which we can see others and judge them and ourselves. (346)

Having established the social role of fiction, Atwood proceeds to define the task of the writer in a way that suggests his role may be considerably broader than that of examiner and chronicler.

I've implied that the writer functions in his or her society as a kind of soothsayer, a truth teller; that writing is not mere self-expression but a view of society and the world at large, and that the novel is a moral instrument. *Moral* implies political, and traditionally the novel has been used not only as a vehicle for social commentary but as a vehicle for political commentary as well. The novelist, at any rate, still sees a connection between politics and the moral sense, even if politicians gave that up some time ago. By "political" I mean having to do with power: who's got it, who wants it, how it operates; in a word, who's allowed to do what to whom, who gets what from whom, who gets away with it and how. (353)

Atwood is careful to deny any desire to see the writer as the servant of a political movement; indeed she views such subordination as destructive of true literary creativity. The writer must reach her or his socio-political conclusions independently and give individual expression to them. Nevertheless, she sees the impossibility of writers working as "totally isolated individuals"; she sees them as "inescapably connected with their society."

> The nature of their connection will vary — the writer may unconsciously reflect the society, he may consciously examine it and project ways of changing it; and the connection between writer and society will increase in intensity as the society (rather than, for instance, the writer's love-life or his meditations on roses) becomes the "subject" of the writer. (*Second Words* 148)

The role of examining society, or providing a moral touchstone demands a high degree of realism in observing the social environment and in rendering it in fictional terms, even though absolute realism is impossible, and facts will always be manipulated for formal reasons or slanted with satiric intent. Nevertheless, a basic respect for the actuality of the world is necessary. "The world exists; the writer testifies," as Atwood says. "She cannot deny anything human." In *Survival* she praises the Canadian writers of the generation before her, like Hugh MacLennan and Margaret Laurence, for "facing the facts, grim though they may be." And the prerequisite of a good novel, she suggests, is that it should be rooted in the visible world, the "real world" as we call it, and out of that rooting its individual blossoms will appear. Discussing fiction about women in a 1978 essay entitled "The Curse of Eve," she remarked:

> There's no shortage of female characters in the literary tradition, and the novelist gets her or his ideas about women from the same sources everyone else does; from the media, books, films, radios, television and newspapers, from home and school, and from the culture at large, the body of received opinion. Also, luckily, sometimes through personal experience which contradicts all of these. (*Second Words* 219)

It is in the early poetry of Margaret Atwood that one is mostly aware of the writer "in love with the language, with the act of creation, with yourself partly," and indeed the language-oriented, private aspect of her outlook continues even now to be more evident in her novel than in her fiction. From her first published novel, *The Edible Woman*, one is aware of the socially concerned writer taking on what she regards as the responsibilities of fiction. She exposes the anomie that characterizes the consumer society and creates a tension in her central character which drives her beyond reason into a life-denying neurosis, out of which she emerges through a descent into the world of sympathetic magic, terminating in an act of ritual cannibalism that verges on symbolic self-immolation. The rational, as exemplified in the tonally flat realism of the narrative and the irony of the protagonist's perceptions, is shown to be perilously linked with psychosis; the coldly thinking mind is also the sick mind. The ancient recourses of myth and magic offer a way out towards sanity.

The same pattern exists in *Surfacing*, where the apparently realistic presentation of the world which Atwood's view of the writers role demands is accompanied by an irrational climax that appears to be its opposite. The extraordinary faithfulness with which at the beginning of the novel Atwood introduces us to the landscape and life of the marginal bushland on the Québec verge of the Canadian Shield has often been praised; here is the land and here are the people, rendered to life. The narrating "I" may be a failed artist, but her perceiving eye is clear, and these sharp notations of the visible world continue throughout her period of surrender of mind and self, so that the seeming madness of her visions is if anything emphasized by the continuing and meticulous description of the background of it all.

Later I shall discuss the climax of the novel in more detail, but here my point is that it leaves us in doubt as to how to describe the novel. Is it throughout a realistic work in which Atwood is carrying out what she believes to be the novelist's duty of describing, in which case the narrator's super-rational experience itself becomes an observed phenomenon? Or are we to regard the book as an exercise in Gothicism, in which details sharply perceived and rendered emphasize the spectral unreality of the narrator's vision by the verisimilitude of their setting?

Atwood confuses us with an explanation of her own, which she offered twice in interviews, with Graeme Gibson in 1973 and later with Linda Sandler in 1974. She tells Gibson — and Sandler also in almost the same words that: "... for me, the interesting thing in that book is the ghost in it, and that's what I like. And the other stuff is there, it's quite true, but it is a condition; it isn't, to me, what the book is about." And a little later, explaining herself, she goes on to talk of ghost stories in general, and adds:

> You can have the Henry James kind, in which the ghost that one sees is in fact a fragment of one's own self which has split off, and that to me is the most interesting kind and that is obviously the tradition I'm working in. (29)

Are we to take Atwood at her word? Or is she perhaps being playful with her interviewers? Are we to conclude that, as so often happens in the case of works of the imagination, there is more to the book than the writer cares to admit? And how can we reconcile the idea of ghost stories, which are usually written to entertain, with Atwood's notion of the broader tasks and duties of the fiction writer? Some answers will emerge from the chapters that follow.

THE STORY AS TOLD

In volume, *Surfacing* is a slight book, by Atwood's as well as other standards; the first Canadian edition consists of 192 pages, compared with 281 pages of *The Edible Woman*, and even more for the later novels. Its structure and its plot complement this brevity with their comparative simplicity. So far as time present is concerned, the duration of the action is slight, just over a week, though false and true memories extend it far into the protagonist's childhood. Again, except in the remembered past, the place of the novel is restricted to a single setting of the lake-dotted north, wild land on the edge of civilization.

The novel is written entirely as a first-person narrative, spoken by the anonymous protagonist, who is "I" to herself and "you" to everyone else, whether or in the past or in the present. She appears at first as a not very competent commercial artist, largely brought up in the bush lands to which she returns for the duration of the novel after an urban life in which she remembers a spoilt marriage, a husband and child deserted, and communication broken for many years with her parents. "By story-telling, we obviously don't mean just the plot," Atwood once said.

It's the timing, isn't it? And the gestures, the embellishments, the tangents, the occasion, the expression on the face of the teller, and whether you like him or not. (*Second Words* 335)

And often, as we read through *Surfacing*, we realise that the way "I" tells them counts more in the story than the actual physical events, for it is what her mind makes of them rather than what might objectively be seen that forms the real substance of the *rite de passage* at the heart of the novel. Even small features of her way of telling become important, such as the fact that she speaks often in run-on sentences which signal the disorder of her mind.

Surfacing falls into three parts, in which external events occur in chronological sequence but the past, clouded by the protagonist's self-protective amnesia, emerges in temporal confusion to take on its true shape. The first part consists of a little over a third of the book, the second occupies almost a half, and the third, the climactic one, consists of a mere 33 pages or just over a sixth of the novel. The first part is told in the present tense; the perceptions are sharp yet the impression is that of a shallow Now, hardly more than two-dimensional, like a pre-Raphaelite painting, and this corresponds to the timeless world, with her real past virtually shut off, in which the narrator is living as the story begins. The second part is told in the past tense, and this corresponds with the Proustian recovery of time lost which precipitates the narrator into her mental crisis. Part three returns her through visions and delusions to speaking in the present tense, but hers is now no longer a present that depends on the exclusion of the past and the denial of the self; it is a present in which the self is renewed and the past accepted and thus outgrown.

The first part begins like a detective story as "I" and her companions find their way, through a childhood landscape changed by time, to the French-Canadian village on the shore of the lake where she spent so much of her childhood; she is accompanied by her laconic lover, Joe, and two crass and casual friends, Dave and Anna. "I" has been told that her father, an eccentric botanist living alone on a lake island, has vanished without a trace, and though she has not been in touch with him for many years, she feels bound to go on an attempt to find what has happened to him.

The early chapters read like a detective story as she first goes to the old *canadien* farmer on the lakeshore who was her father's only friend among the local people, and then, reaching the island, carefully checks over the house for clues that might suggest a reason for his disappearance. She finds everything in apparent order, and then leads her companions in a fruitless search of the paths of the island, half obliterated by vegetation. There is no trace of the missing man, and as his boats are all safely on the island, she does not know where to search. She seems reconciled to abandoning the effort.

> No one can expect anything else from me. I checked everything, I tried; now I'm absolved from knowing. I should be telling someone official, filling in forms, getting help you're supposed to in an emergency. But it's like searching for a ring lost on a beach or in the snow: futile. There's no act I can perform except waiting; tomorrow Evans will ship us to the village, and after that we'll travel to the city and the present tense. I've finished what I came for and I don't want to stay here, I want to go back to where there is electricity and distraction. I'm used to it now, filling the time without it is an effort. (51)

The present tense of the cities, of modern life, the absolution from "knowing," are of course protections from and also of the past, the real past of which she is uneasily becoming aware again on the island; she is already becoming restless, indulging in fits of retrospection in which she sees herself as a head detached from the body (an image already used in Atwood's poetry) — cerebral, unfeeling, separated from a lost real self.

But she does not return immediately to the city, since her companions decided that they would like to stay another week on the island and she unwillingly agrees. It is now, in the second part of the novel, that she discovers the evidence which changes the nature of the quest. With time on her hands after the blueberry picking and fishing expeditions with which she entertains the others, she searches among the relics of her parents' life that are left in the house. She finds her mother's albums of photographs, and the scrapbooks she and her brother used to keep, hers full of sentimentalized animal drawings and cutouts of women's dresses, his of grim scenes of war. Memories flow in, as they do with recovering amnesiacs, each clue that evokes a memory leading by association to the memory of another concealed incident, another episode perceived with fear and dreamlike luminosity. She finds herself becoming inexplicably intolerant of some of her more recent memories, like that of her marriage and the husband and child she deserted.

And then she turns back to the strange drawings she had already discovered when she was rummaging among her father's papers in search of a possible message: crude drawings of anthropoids and strange creatures with hastily scrawled comments. She sees them on that first encounter with a sense of shock and apprehension.

> That's what he was doing here all winter, he was shut up in this cabin making these unintelligible drawings. I sit at the table, my heart speeded up as if I've opened up what I thought was an empty closet and found myself face to face with a thing that isn't supposed to be there, like a claw or a bone. This is the forgotten possibility: he might have gone insane. Crazy, loony. Bushed, the trappers call it when you stay in the forest by yourself too long. And if insane, perhaps not dead: none of the rules would be the same. (60)

It is from this point that the haunting begins, though not yet in ghostly terms, for it is the appearance out of hiding of her father himself, "like a huge ragged moth" and mad, that she fears. When she does agree to stay, she goes searching for a will or some other document that might declare his intentions. Having searched everywhere else, she comes to the strange drawings. As she looks through them again, their outlandish character increasingly convinces her of her father's insanity. "Total derangement," she concludes. "The drawing was something he saw, a hallucination; or it might have been himself, what he thought he was turning into" (101).

Her assumptions are shattered when she comes across a letter from an archaeological researcher thanking her father for the material he has been sending regarding Indian rock paintings. He had remained sane — and therefore must be dead. But even when she has reached this conclusion she is moved by a morbidly compelling curiosity to follow the indications of a map she finds, with markings that correspond to the drawings.

She goes out secretly, dives before one of the cliffs and, instead of seeing an Indian painting, is confronted by a body floating under the surface. It is in fact the body of her father, as searchers later confirm, weighed down by the heavy camera he has been carrying slung around his neck, and this she must subconsciously know. But at the moment of shock it is the embryo of the child she had aborted in the deliberately forgotten past that suddenly comes back to her with traumatic vigour. Her marriage, and the husband and child she abandoned, never existed; they were fabrications brought on by her guilt over what had really happened, when the middle-aged professor who was her lover persuaded her to get rid of the child she might have had by him. This guilt, she realizes, was the real reason why she had not dared to continue seeing her parents, the reason why she created the cool, ironic surrogate self she takes with her to the lake.

Now, obsessively, moving like a person in trance whom she herself observes from outside, she sets out to shed the false self she had acquired, to unlearn adulthood and return through her childhood, to go beyond humanity and attain the animal condition, near to the gods, as she does in the third part of the book.

The extra week has drawn to an end. She has persuaded her lover Joe to impregnate her (as she hopes confidently), so that the lost child can finally be born. When the boat arrives to take the party back to the village, she runs away from her companions. After they have departed, she lives naked on the island, observing a strange pattern of taboos that comes into her mind, and inducing the weakness that brings on hallucinations by living — barely living — on roots and mushrooms. She sees her mother like a ghost and in her father's place the monster she fears he has become. But afterwards she goes to the place where the monster had stood and sees footprints; she steps into them and realizes they are her own. That night she dreams she sees her parents departing, paddling in their old green canoe out of the island's bay.

> When I wake in the morning I know they have gone finally, back into the earth, the air, the water, wherever they were when I summoned them. The rules are over. I can go anywhere now, into the cabin, into the garden, I can walk on the paths. I am the only one left alive on the island. (188)

The delirium that is panic in a double sense — fear and godly intervention — has passed away from her. The gods she sought have appeared and departed. She is alone, with the child she now wants growing in her womb. As the novel draws to an end, a boat comes up to the dock. It is old Paul's battered launch, and Joe is in it. He comes ashore, and calls her name, the first time it is called in the book.

She thinks: "[H]e's here, a mediator, an ambassador, offering me something: captivity in any of its forms, a new freedom?" And she concludes that "he isn't an American, I can see that now; he isn't anything, he is only half-formed, and for that reason I can trust him." Still, by the time the book ends she has not made up her mind to join him; her feet have not moved. "The lake is quiet, the trees surround me, asking and giving nothing" (192).

One senses, in this ending which Atwood has admitted is deliberately ambiguous, that benign indifference of the universe of which Albert Camus spoke often. There is not hope, but there is sanity, a courageous coming into the light of reality, a sense that what she does is less important than what she is — the self she has rediscovered along with her real past.†

THE METAPHORICAL STRUCTURE

Surfacing is structurally bound together not only by its chronological pattern of action, but also by its patterns of clustered metaphors. They relate, on the most obvious level, to the title of the book, images of submersion and coming up for air, of drownings and near drownings, which become the metaphors of the ego searching for the self in the depths of the unconscious. Closely connected with this dominant metaphorical cluster is that associated with birth and death and especially with the embryo; the link between these two clusters is made clear when "I" remarks of her aborted child that "it had

---

† Readers whose minds are tuned to detective stories may notice here — though to my knowledge no critic has so far done so — the small mystery trap that Atwood has playfully laid for us. When "I" gets to the village, Paul, her father's friend, tells her that the "boats are there," and she answers, "If the boats are there he can't have gone off the island" (23). Yet the cliff before which she sees his body floating is definitely off the island and somewhere on the lake shore. It would have needed a boat to reach it. If it was this cliff on which her father cracked his skull, how did he get there and still leave all his boats on the island? Did some mysterious person who has never appeared take him there and push him over? Or are we to assume that he fell off a cliff on his own island (where no pictographic sites are shown on his map and there were probably no paintings to be seen) and that his body drifted across the lake to the cliff? It sounds unlikely. The question is left open and nobody has picked it up.

drowned in air." Linked to both the submersion-surfacing images, which can involve drowning but also rising into the light, and to the birth images which emphasize the perilous existence of the unborn being (and by extension of the unrealized self), is the further metaphorical cluster consisting of the people and animals who in various ways become the metaphors of survival, which of course was one of Atwood's main concerns at the time she was writing *Surfacing*, and the subject of *Survival*, the other book she published in 1972.

Finally, less obviously connected with the main cluster of metaphors, but equally essential to the business of the novel, is the group of metaphors that emerges from what Marge Piercy has called "the notion of pictures, from pictographs to childhood drawings (personal pictographs), the camera, the illustrations the heroine does for pseudo-European fairy tales" (McCombs 63).

Among the submersion-surfacing episodes most neglected by critics are the fishing expeditions undertaken by the visiting Americans or pseudo-Americans and also by "I" and her companions. Dragged from their natural element, the fish, like the aborted child, drown in air if they are not expertly killed beforehand by "I" with her blows at the neck. Repeatedly through the novel we are reminded of the difference between natural predation, including that of the native hunter, on the one hand, and the predation of the white man, American or other, fishing for pleasure, which mainly consists of the excitement of killing. This contributes to what is one of the central themes of the book, the alienation of modern man, unlike his aboriginal predecessors, from the natural world and natural ways of living.

The first of the three most striking submersion episodes is that in which the narrator's brother escapes as a small child from the pen his father had constructed for him, and falls into the lake, whence his mother rescues him at the last moment. The brother, whom we encounter only indirectly, through the narrator's memory, a few photographs, and his scrapbook, is one of the most interesting and enigmatic presences in the novel. In a sense, while escaping drowning, he has not escaped from submersion. Having cut himself off from his parents even before his sister, he now lives in Australia, Down Under, working as a prospector, which means penetrating down into the earth, another kind of submergence.

In the narrative he appears as "I" 's opposite, the dark other side to their father's rationalism. Their scrapbooks reveal their differences.

I didn't want there to be wars and death, I wanted them not to exist; only rabbits with their coloured egg houses, sun and moon orderly above the flat earth, summer always, I wanted everyone to be happy. But his pictures were more accurate, the weapons, the disintegrating soldiers: he was a realist, that protected him. He almost drowned once but he would never allow that to happen again, by the time he left he was ready. (131)

It is the brother who always knowingly discovers and reveals the unpleasant aspects of life from which their islanded childhood had protected the two, and transmits them to his sister. It is he in whom a boyhood cruelty, as complete as Golding reveals in *Lord of the Flies*, emerges as he traps wild creatures and then leaves them to die. "I" sometimes releases them until she becomes scared of his anger. "Because of my fear they were killed." Remembering it all, she reflects:

It wasn't the city that was wrong, the inquisitors in the school-yard, we weren't better than they were; we just had different victims. To become a little child again, a barbarian, a vandal: it was in us too, it was innate. A thing closed in my head, hand, synapse, cutting off my escape: that was the wrong way, the entrance, redemption was elsewhere, I must have overlooked it. (132)

Her father submerges, but is never rescued, being in the end hooked by stray fishermen and dragged from the water a decomposing barely recognizable corpse. He seems to have died accidentally, seeking actual pictographs, since he had his camera with him. "I" assumes that through observing the pictographs, her father had begun to be affected by the beliefs they represented.

The Indians did not own salvation but they had once known where it lived and their signs marked the sacred places, the places where you could learn the truth. . . . He had discovered new places, new oracles, they were things he was seeing the way I had seen, true vision; at the end, after the failure of logic. (145)

And despite what she has seen, the corpse in the water, she refuses to accept the reality of his death, and believes David is lying when he brings the message from the party that came to the island with the news of the discovery of his body. For her he has already become the ghostly guide in the personal quest she must undertake, and not until it is complete can she believe he is dead, perhaps for the *hubris* of those who seek the gods too relentlessly. For it is as a metaphor of rationality defeated that his death haunts the book.

In the case of the narrator there are two submersions. The first of them is the series of dives, in search of pictographs, in the last of which she sees her father's body, and then, as she surfaces, catches sight of the "green canoe . . . far above me, sunlight radiating around it," and perceives it as "a beacon, safety" (142). And, indeed, her surfacing is an anticipation of her self integration, a beacon leading towards fulfillment. But only an anticipation; the real process takes place later on, and this too includes an act of submersion which is a kind of sacrifice, and presumably an acceptable one. At the height of her trance-like experience the narrator goes down to the beach, after she has destroyed as a preliminary sacrifice everything that can be burnt or broken in her parents' house. She lies down in the water, completely immersing herself, peels off her clothes and stays there naked.

> My back is on the sand, my head rests against the rock, innocent as plankton; my hair spreads out, moving and fluid in the water. The earth rotates, holding my body down to it as it holds the moon; the sun pounds in the sky, red flames and rays pulsing from it, searing away the wrong form that encases me, dry rain soaking through me, warming the blood egg I carry. I dip my head beneath the water, washing my eyes.
>
> Inshore a loon; it lowers its head, then lifts it again and calls. It sees me but it ignores me, accepts me as part of the land.
>
> When I am clean I come up out of the lake, leaving my false body floated on the surface, a cloth decoy; it jiggles in the waves I make, nudges gently against the dock.
>
> They offered clothing as a token, formerly; that was partial but the gods are demanding, absolute, they want all. (177–78)

Submersion, in this final manifestation, has become baptism, which is normally seen as the prelude to spiritual transformation, but here preludes psychological transformation.

The birth metaphors in *Surfacing* are linked to the submersion metaphors in the sense that the embryo is kept alive by its submersion in the fluids of the womb, and drowns in air if it is not allowed its proper cycle of growth there until the moment of birth, which is a kind of surfacing. Hence the heroine's guilt because of allowing her child to be aborted. In preventing birth she has prevented life, and in the process she has locked herself into a circle of guilt which is a kind of death, and from which she awaits the release of inner rebirth.

For the narrator the embryo not only represents potentiality, as it does for all of us, but potency also; it has powers that exceed those of nature. When she writes of her brother's near drowning while their mother was pregnant with her, she tells:

> It was before I was born but I can remember it as clearly as if I saw it, and perhaps I did see it: I believe that an unborn baby has its eyes open and can look out through the walls of the mother's stomach, like a frog in a jar. (32)

Later, as she moves towards her psychological crisis, and had assumed that her father's drawings of the Indian pictographs contain some special message for her which she must identify and interpret, she assumes that her dead mother must have left a message too. She searches in the house and finds yet another scrapbook of her early childhood drawings of people with "hairs blazing out of their heads like rays or spikes, and suns with faces." There is also "a loose page, the edge torn, the figures drawn in crayon," and this she regards as her mother's gift to her.

> On the left was a woman with a round moon stomach: the baby was sitting up inside her gazing out. Opposite her was a man with horns on his head like cow horns and a barbed tail.
> The picture was mine, I had made it. The baby was myself before I was born, the man was God, I'd drawn him when my brother learned in the winter about the Devil and God: if the Devil was allowed a tail and horns, God needed them also, they were advantages. (158)

But such manifestations of infant Manicheism, with God and Devil contending as equals, must be replaced by new meanings which she had to learn by immersing herself in "another language."

The association of the embryo with the frog in the earlier quotation is the first of a number of comparisons between foetuses and frogs

41

which remind one that in the shamanistic cults of Canadian Indians the frog was regarded as a magically powerful creature, to be respected and feared. Similarly, at the end of the book, "I" sees the embryo she hopes is growing inside her as a being of special quality, a "time-traveller," with the "untravelled paths" "potential already in its proto-brain." It is "no god," but it might be "the first one, the first true human; it must be born, allowed" (191).

Finally, the idea of surfacing as expressed in the novel is closely linked with the idea of survival as projected in the book of that title. *Survival* teaches that people or animals in danger of submersion (or its equivalent, extinction) must struggle to preserve themselves, to stay, as it were, on the surface. Otherwise they become victims, and *Survival* consists largely of elaborate descriptions of victim types and victim situations as they appear in Canadian literature, especially fiction and poetry. The preoccupation with victimization spills over into *Surfacing*, and among its fauna are many of the victim types described in *Survival*. As significant figures, part metaphor and part character, there appear victim animals (a heron and some fish and frogs), victim Indians (it is too far south for victim Inuit), victim sham pioneers (it is too late in history for real ones), victim children, victim artists (the chapter heading — "The Paralysed Artist" — in *Survival* perfectly describes Joe the frustrated potter in *Surfacing*), victim women, and victim French Canadians. That leaves out four categories featured in *Survival*: victim explorers, victim immigrants, victim heroes, and victim jail-breakers. But it may be a point in the novel that the narrator contains all these missing roles, since she is an explorer of her own past, she is a migrant into a new self, she is as much a heroine — and a martyred one — as the novel permits, and she is breaking the jail of her imprisoned spirit. In other words, she is moving as the novel ends into "Position Four" of *Survival*, "*To be a creative non-victim*," in which "creative activity of all kinds becomes possible" and "you are able to accept your own experience for what it is, rather than having to distort it to correspond with others' versions of it . . ." (*Survival* 38–39).

The remaining metaphorical cluster in *Surfacing* stands somewhat apart from the three I have just discussed, all of which in some way support the novel's major metaphor of submersion and surfacing. These are the drawings and photographs which are not only images, but enter into the narrative in a double way — as metaphors that project the mental life of the narrator, but also as objects which affect the action.

The narrator herself is an artist of sorts, though a frustrated one like her potter lover Joe; while he produces deliberately distorted and mutilated pots in an attempt to achieve some kind of originality, she earns her living making drawings to illustrate books for children, and particularly European fairy tales that have no place in Canada's mythology. We have already noted the crucial role of her father's drawings of Indian pictographs in precipitating her crisis; later, as we shall see, the images from native mythology will influence the course the crisis takes. The drawings they execute in childhood reflect the differing minds of the narrator and her brother, his acceptance of the existence of evil, leading to a profession that involves the violating of the earth, and her failure to shed a sentimentalized view of existence which has prevented her from facing evil when she encountered it.

All the drawings mentioned in *Surfacing*, whether they are by children or by "I" as a would-be professional, aimed at diverting rather than intensifying one's sense of reality. And something very similar applies to the father's attempts to reproduce Indian pictographs, since these are rendered in the spirit of scientific enquiry whereas the originals were done in the spirit of religious awe. Their falseness as works of art mirrors the falseness of the view of life presented by their practitioners, and in the case of the narrator shows how early, in her drawings of rabbits living in eggshell houses, she began to retreat from reality, about which she had to be told by her more knowing brother.

Cameras and photography play a crucial role in both the action and the metaphorical structure of *Surfacing*. Albums of photographs in the cabin enable the narrator to recover large areas of her past that she has almost wilfully forgotten, and this prepares for the re-emergence of her true self at the end of the novel.

Joe and David, the male companions of her trip to the island, bring a movie camera.

> They're making a movie, Joe is doing the camera work, he's never done it before but David says they're the new Renaissance Men, you teach yourself what you need to learn. It was mostly David's idea, he calls himself the director: they already have the credits worked out. He wants to get shots of things they come

across, random samples he calls them, and that will be the name of the movie too: *Random Samples*. When they've used up their supply of film (which was all they could afford; and the camera is rented) they're going to look at what they've collected and rearrange it. (10)

In a different form, *Random Samples* shows the same kind of false perception as the drawings, for it is an effort by two men who uneasily perceive the falsity of modern life, even though they are deeply immersed in it, and seek to exploit its discrepancies and incongruities in this film which has neither continuity nor any clear relation, critical or otherwise, to the world whose fragments it so desultorily records. The very act of filming becomes a negation, an offense against life, when David uses it deliberately to humiliate his wife Anna and proposes to humiliate the narrator in the same way. It is significant that "I"'s first overt action of rejecting her recent past and its world should be the dumping of the undeveloped film into the lake, and hence its destruction. Having done this, she vanishes just before the boat comes to take the party back to the village.

A camera, of course, plays an equally negative role in the case of her father, weighing him down when he falls in the water so that he drowns. The suggestion, never drawn out to anything more specific, is that he dies because he approached the sacred sites of the pictographs in the spirit of logical enquiry instead of the spirit of reverence; he has died for the *hubris* of modern man.

If we seek to penetrate the metaphorical implications of this series of graphic and photographic images, and of the acts of producing them, I suggest we have to regard them as a demonstration that bad art is a product and a sign of the unintegrated personality, the unintegrated life. One is reminded — though Atwood may not have intended this — of Herbert Read's argument in *Education through Art*, that if children are encouraged to pursue their artistic impulses, they will find their lives taking on the harmony they themselves create in form and colour. Bad art, in other words, goes hand in hand with a false way of living, and to change our way of living we must recover our true and clear images of reality as in the end the narrator does.

44

If on any point there is broad agreement among the critics who have written on *Surfacing*, it is on the inadequacies of Atwood's characterization. Her treatment of the people in her novels has been dismissed as "shallow," and the characters themselves regarded as thematic vehicles, "illustrating social theories rather than having fictional lives of their own." And the fact is that compared with Margaret Laurence's, Atwood's do seem thin and in their ways unmatured.

Partly this is due to the strength of the thematic direction of the novel, which is concerned with the problem of self-realization and self-liberation already discussed on another level in the almost simultaneously published *Survival*. And here I think we might consider with some profit a remark Marge Piercy throws off in passing during her discussion of Atwood's fiction. "I wonder if the protagonist in *Surfacing* has no name because she has not, till the end of the novel, earned one" (McCombs 63).

"I," in fact, is a voice rather than a character when the novel begins, the voice of a lost personality which finds its identity as the story proceeds; unlike the Laurencian novel which, in *The Stone Angel* and *The Diviners* for example, reveals an already developed character from the beginning, largely dominating the action, in *Surfacing* the action shapes and finally releases the character. This is one reason for the importance of the foetal imagery. The characters for whom there is hope grow like embryos as the novel proceeds, towards the liberation of a kind of birth. The narrator reaches it, and there is a good chance, we feel, that Joe will do so; David and Anna are locked into patterns of action and reaction from which there seems to be no escape.

Characterization, it is clear, does not have the same primary function for Margaret Atwood as it does for Margaret Laurence. It is not the reason for existence of the novel, with the characters taking on lives of their own, and the themes, such as they are, emerging from the characters' actions and their reactions to the world around.

Not that Atwood's characters are indifferent to the world. They are deeply involved in it in their own ways. Sherrill Grace has made the illuminating remark that in *Surfacing*, as in some of her poems, Atwood views the self as "a place or entity co-extensive with its environment" (Grace 2). This is so on the more obvious level that throughout the novel the narrator feels herself to be hurt by whatever harm she sees done to the environment, and it is so on the deeper level when she seeks her liberation through a regression to primitiveness which involves total immersion in the environment to the extent of shedding her human characteristics for the time being, even speech.

Here we are clearly at a level where thematic considerations operate and the character is rather obviously — "artificially" it has seemed to some critics — being shaped by the author's ideas about the conflict between natural man and civilized man as he exists in contemporary North America. One never has the sense, as one does from the first page of *The Stone Angel*, that the character has taken on a life of her own and is almost dragging the author behind her. Atwood always seems in firm control of her characters, and there is never the sense that she has been immersed in the life of the being she has created. Perhaps her attitude is best stated in the last sentence of a 1982 essay ("Writing the Male Character").

> If writing novels — and reading them — have any redeeming social value, it's probably that they force you to imagine what it's like to be somebody else. (*Second Words* 430)

You don't feel that you *are* the character; you *imagine what it's like to be* him or her, which is a very different thing.

In the light of what I have said about Atwood's attitude towards characters and characterization, let us take a closer look at the figures who inhabit *Surfacing*. Only seven of the characters, four living and three dead or departed and therefore observed through the distorting lens of memory, are of real importance. The idiosyncracies of the four living ones are emphasized by the fact that they are living for the present of the novel in close quarters on the island, and so are constantly reacting to each other and exposed to the narrator's ironic observation. The other characters, the French-Canadian shopkeepers and resort owners of the village and the Americans who corrupt them, are shallowly sketched to fit their minor roles in the action; we see them only briefly through the narrator's eyes, and they never have time even to develop as humours.

The two parents, though neither of them appears in the present of the novel as a living person, are more important in terms of the novel's development than any of the living characters except the narrator herself. She tends in memory to idealize and simplify then, and to explain her avoidance of them after her abortion in somewhat conventional terms of good and evil. She has known evil, they have not.

> They never knew, about that or why I left. Their own innocence, the reason why I couldn't tell them; perilous innocence, closing them in glass, their artificial garden, greenhouse. They didn't teach us about evil, they didn't understand about it, how could I describe it to them? They were from another age, prehistoric, when everyone got married and had a family, children growing in the yard like sunflowers; remote as Eskimoes or mastodons. (144)

This does not entirely agree with her accounts of the parents when other memories come up, and particularly of her father as misanthropist with an inclination towards reclusion who has seen enough of life to make him distrust and despise most of humankind and to prefer the animals because they are more "rational." In fact, it seems to have been largely because of fear of a world about which they knew a great deal in one way or another, that the parents erred in bringing up the narrator to be so ignorant of life beyond the home and the island that she must learn about it in shameful indirection from her more knowing and, by implication, her more corrupt brother.

Of course, her attempts to dismiss her parents, whether in the past or in the present of the book, are unsuccessful, for it was they who shaped her and who nurtured the contradictions that become evident as we slowly learn about her past. Both of them have explicitly or implicitly rejected civilization and its alleged benefits, though their commitment to life in the wilds is no more complete than Thoreau's, who could always walk from Walden into Concord to enjoy the amenities; they live over winter in the cities, and then their children go to urban schools. Still, the mystique of the natural life is there, finding expression in the case of her father — a 19th-century scientific materialist — through logic, for the animal world he has committed himself to study becomes in his view a model for human beings to follow. Her mother's reaction is more intuitive, for at times she wanders in the woods as if entranced, and develops an active empathy towards animals, so that she can stand still for long periods and the jays will come to settle on her arms and shoulders and eat the food she holds in her hands; she can stand in front of bears, shouting at them, and they will go away. And yet, even in their home in the wilds, the parents are willing to discipline nature in ways that have existed since neolithic man first hoed a patch of earth and sowed the seeds of wild grass; they expand great effort, for example, in cultivating a patch of land.

> It took them years to make the garden, the real soil was too sandy and anaemic. This oblong was artificial, the product of skill and of compost spaded in, black muck dredged from swamps, horse dung ferried by boat from the winter logging camps when they still kept horses to drag the logs to the frozen lake. My father and mother would carry it in bushel baskets on the handbarrow, two poles with boards nailed across, each of them lifting an end. (78)

The relationship between a character and her name is evident, and even when the novelist or dramatist does not, like Dickens, pick a name that immediately seems to reflect the leading traits of the character, we still find that name and personality by the end of the novel or play have been so closely integrated that a mere mention of the name evokes the personality and his qualities. Hamlet, for example, is a name drawn out of folk history, so neutral in its connotations that, apart from Shakespeare's play, it would evoke nothing in the common reader's mind. But since Shakespeare did write the play we have only to mention the name for melancholic indecision to appear personified before us.

Thus a character without a name is hardly a character at all, and it is so that the narrator appears at the beginning of *Surfacing*, as a voice rather than a person. We are impressed immediately by the cool tone of that voice and also by the sharp ironic mind it seems to project, a mind that shrewdly perceives others and penetrates beneath the surface to observe the way their minds work, to assess their motives. But behind the perceiving eye and the superficial rationality of her mental process, which she clearly inherits from her father, we slowly become aware of an unintegrated mind and nature. We recognize the violent dominating prejudice that distorts her perceptions (and ours to begin with), according to which she sees everything American as evil, refusing to acknowledge the offences against nature and life of her fellow Canadians, so that, conversely, everything evil is American. We notice also, as Linda Hutcheon has pointed out, "a discrepancy between narrative tone and actual event," for gradually we realize that we are being told in a cool, collected voice about events, both in the mind and outside it, that a normal person would find highly disturbing. And we realize that however much of mental alertness "I" has inherited or acquired from her father, she is emotionally undeveloped; she sees herself increasingly, as the novel continues, as a head detached from its body (or mental activity detached from the senses and the feelings), and this distancing of her mind from the reality of her life has enabled her to create the false past — and therefore the false persona — that her irrational guilt demands. The reunion of mind and body, the cleansing of the memory, will be achieved through the *rite de passage* which is the novel's dénouement and which will signal "I" 's development into a true character worthy of a name.

In most novels we gain our knowledge about the characters at least partly through the way they are reflected by the other characters who help to define them by reacting to them; they act, in other words, like the side mirrors of an old dressing table, multiplying and varying the image which the character creates when he is seen full face. But one of the ideas that obsesses the narrator in *Surfacing* is that of the mirrors that have ceased to reflect, or at least to reflect her, and two of her three companions, David and Anna, are almost like non-reflecting mirrors — shallow surfaces that contain no image from outside.

On a cruder level there are obvious resemblances between the narrator and David. He does not have the verbal facility with which she speaks, though one feels this is a quality he has deliberately abandoned; can he always have spoken in the wornout jargon of the counterculture? But he has an ironic perception not unlike hers, and she recognizes the amoral similarity between them.

David is like me, I thought, we are the ones that don't know how to love, there is something essentially missing in us, we are born that way. (*Surfacing* 14)

Yet, like as they are, she will not couple with David when he pursues her, and we are perhaps free to interpret this refusal as part of her awakening to the other half that lives deep within her and must achieve its liberating metamorphosis. It is, significantly, at this time, when she rejects him sexually, that she first sees him as he is, and also sees him as in some way a parody of the self she has become and needs to discard.

> The power flowed into my eyes, I could see into him, he was an imposter, a pastiche, layers of political handbills, pages from magazines, *affiches*, verbs and nouns glued on to him and shredding away, the original surface littered with fragments and tatters. In a black suit knocking on doors, young once, even that had been a costume, a uniform; now his hair was falling off and he didn't know what language to use, he'd forgotten his own, he had to copy. Second-hand American was spreading over him in patches, like mange or lichen. He was infested, garbled, and I couldn't help him: it would take such time to heal, unearth him, scrape down to where he was true. (152)

This recognition — at least on a conscious level — comes only towards the end of the novel; earlier on, when they first reach the island, she is willing to identify ironically with David and Anna.

> A little beer, a little pot, some jokes, a little political chitchat, the golden mean; we're the new bourgeoisie, this might as well be a Rec Room. Still I'm glad they're with me, I wouldn't want to be here alone; at any moment the loss, vacancy, will overtake me, they ward it off. (39)

Yet as she begins to move towards her self-realization, she deliberately flees from their company, and in the end of the novel, when her mind is purged of delusions, she sits in the island house, eating beans out of a can and thinks:

> David and Anna were here, they slept in the far bedroom; I remember them, but indistinctly and with nostalgia, as I remember people I once knew. They live in the city now, in a different time. (188)

Anna is hardly a character at all, for she has hardly more depth than the transforming makeup she applies to her pallid features every morning, convinced that in an emotional way David will punish her if she does not. She is, rather, a type, projecting one of the book's minor themes, which is the subjection of women, though there is a deliberate ambivalence here, in the suggestion that her relationship with David, a relationship that at first seems to be one of domination and subordination, is also one of complicity between victor and victim.

> I remembered what Anna had said about emotional commitments: they've made one, I thought, they hate each other; that must be almost as absorbing as love. (138)

There remains Joe, the most enigmatic character in the book; is he deep or is he just dumb? We wonder to the end, and then we suspect but are not quite sure that, like the narrator, he has been going through some process of inner awakening that finally comes manifest in his actions. With his "amorphous beard," which is "just a style now" as "I" remarks, he might be another belated hippy. But there is a self-absorbed, withdrawn quality that distinguishes him from the extroverted David, in whose absurd pranks he becomes a willing accomplice, rather like a small boy admiringly imitating an admired teenager. He is vulnerable, as the narrator recognizes, and indeed at the beginning of the novel she describes him in such a way that he appears not only as the artist as victim, but also as a version of the animal victim, who looks "like the buffalo on the U.S. nickel, shaggy and blunt-snouted, with small clenched eyes and the defiant but insane look of a species once dominant, now threatened with extinction" (8).

Joe is inward-turned, often "off in the place where he spends most of his time," almost incapable of expressing himself in words, and compulsively producing only contorted monstrosities with his hands when he turns to pottery. And yet, unlike David and Anna, he is one for whom the narrator sees a hope of escape from his victimhood.

> For him truth might still be possible, what will preserve him is the absence of words; but the others are already turning to metal, skins galvanizing, heads congealing to brass knobs, components and intricate wires ripening inside. (159)

His bumbling, inarticulate professions of love, we realize, represent a genuine devotion, an emotion of which the other characters have become incapable. The narrator uses it, with the ruthlessness of her own inner urge towards fulfilment, when she virtually forces him to impregnate her; her involvement in the search for liberation from her guilt over the abortion has turned her temporarily into that being dreaded by modern males, the woman as predator. Obviously, without speaking, he senses her needs; he is there when she surfaces from seeing her dead father floating in the lake; it is he, alone, who comes back in old Paul's boat at the end of the novel and calls her name. The last sentences of the novel, all but the final one, are about him.

> But he isn't an American, I can see that now; he isn't anything, he is only half-formed, and for that reason I can trust him.
> To trust is to let go. I tense forward, towards the demands and questions, though my feet do not move yet.
> He calls for me again, balancing on the dock which is neither land nor water, hands on hips, head thrown back and eyes scanning. His voice is annoyed: he won't wait much longer. But right now he waits. (192)

We too wait, expectant, gazing into the benign lakescape. The heroine has not yet made her decision. But her parents have, as her dream tells, departed. The past is no longer a ghost to be exorcised. It is with Joe, the "half-formed," that life can go on and, most readers feel, will go on.

AMBIGUOUS THEMES

No novel that deserves the name is entirely didactic; the elements of real existence, not to mention the writer's imagination, are there to balance and modify the social idea which the action may suggest. And so, compared with a polemical pamphlet, a work of fiction written with some didactic intent can often project a critical, even a contradictory view of one or more of the leading themes. This is certainly the case with *Surfacing*, particularly when one compares it with the openly polemical book of criticism, *Survival*, written at roughly the same time, with its view of Canadian literary culture as being highly distorted by the sickness of colonialism.

52

Essentially, one can observe two major thematic currents running and interlacing through *Surfacing*. One is really an elaboration of an idea which Atwood presented in *Survival* when she was analysing the changing attitudes towards the environment shown by Canadian writers from pioneer days onward.

A curious thing starts happening in Canadian literature once man starts winning, once evidence starts piling up of what Frye in *The Bush Garden* calls "the conquest of nature by an intelligence that does not love it." Sympathy begins to shift from the victorious hero to the defeated giantess, and the problem is no longer how to avoid being swallowed up by a cannibalistic Nature but how to avoid destroying her. (*Survival* 60)

There is no doubt where Atwood stands in *Surfacing*; irrevocably on the side of the assaulted giantess. The narrative is constantly drawing attention to the way in which the landscape has been repeatedly ravaged and robbed.

We're on the trail inside the forest; the first part is fairly open, though now and then we pass gigantic stumps, level and saw-cut, remnants of the trees that were here before the district was logged out. The trees will never be allowed to grow that tall again, they're killed as soon as they're valuable, big trees are scarce as whales. (46)

The lakes have already been raised by making dams, and at places are edged by marshes of stale and standing water that have accumulated around the skeletons of trees which died when the water rose. When they go on fishing expeditions from lake to lake, the narrator and her companions encounter surveyors who are felling trees so that they can plot out a further raising of the lake that will kill yet more of the life along its shoreline.

But the most stark symbol of what man has been wreaking on nature is the heron.

It was behind me, I smelled it before I saw it; then I heard the flies. The smell was like decaying fish. I turned around and it was hanging upside down by a thin blue nylon rope tied round its feet and looped over a tree branch, its wings fallen open. It looked at me with its mashed eye. (115)

For the narrator the issue of the ravaging of the wilderness is simplified by blaming it on the Americans, whom she has known from childhood as "others." In one of her more autobiographical pieces Margaret Atwood recollected:

I spent a large part of my childhood in northern Quebec, surrounded by many trees and few people. My attitude towards Americans was formed by this environment. Alas, the Americans we encountered were usually pictures of ineptitude. We once met two of them dragging a heaving metal boat, plus the motor, across a portage from one lake to another because they did not want to paddle. Typically American, we thought, as they ricocheted off yet another tree. Americans hooked other people when they tried to cast, got lost in the woods and didn't burn their garbage. Of course, many Canadians behaved this way too; but somehow not *as* many. (*Second Words* 375)

The incident described in this passage is virtually reproduced in *Surfacing* when the narrator, encountering what she thinks are American fishermen, remembers her childhood on the lake.

We used to think they were harmless and funny and inept and faintly lovable, like President Eisenhower. We met two of them once on the way to the bass lake, they were carrying their tin motorboat and the motor over the portage so they wouldn't have to paddle once they were on the inner lake; when we first heard them thrashing along through the underbrush we thought they were bears. (66)

But then she finds that the men who had evidently killed the heron and whom she assumed must be Americans, are in fact Canadians who have comically taken her party, with David's long hair, for American late hippies. She is "furious with them, they'd disguised themselves." And she goes on to reflect:

But they'd killed the heron anyway. It doesn't matter what country they're from, my head said, they're still Americans, they're what's in store for us, what we are turning into. They spread themselves like a virus, they get into the brain and take over the cells and the cells change from inside and the ones that have the disease can't tell the difference. Like the late show sci-fi movies, creatures from outer space, body snatchers injecting themselves into you dispossessing your brain, their eyes blank eggshells behind the dark glasses. If you look like them and talk like them and think like them then you are them, I was saying, you speak their language, a language is everything you do. (129)

For her Americans are part of the same evil people she thought were destroyed when Hitler died. "It was like cutting up a tapeworm, the pieces grew."

In passages like this, when the evident paranoia of the still un-regenerated narrator is evident, we begin to recognize how the novel tends to balance the polemics of *Survival*. The narrator may plausibly be regarded as externalising the evil she finds within herself, the evil inherent in the human condition, but in its extremity her statement also emerges as a kind of self-mockery of the Atwood who wrote elsewhere with such passion on the issue of Canada's colonization. A desire to disassociate herself from political stances appears here and also in the passage earlier in the novel when David starts ranting in the tone of Robin Mathews, and even the narrator thinks him naïve for his talk of American invasion and guerilla resistance.

"What war?" I asked, and Anna said "Here we go."

"It's obvious. They're running out of water, clean water, they're dirtying up all of theirs, right? Which is what we have a lot of, this country is almost all water if you look at a map. So in a while, I give it ten years, they'll be up against the wall. They'll try to swing a deal with the government, get us to give them the water cheap or for nothing in exchange for more soapflakes or something, and the government will give in, they'll be a bunch of puppets as usual. But by that time the Nationalist Movement will be strong enough so they'll force the government to back down; riots or kidnappings or something. Then the Yank pigs will send in the Marines, they'll have to; people in New York and Chicago will be dropping like flies, industry will be stalled, there'll be a black market in water, they'll be shipping it in tankers from Alaska. They'll come in through Quebec, it will have separated by then; the Pepsis will even help them, they'll be having a good old laugh. They'll hit the big cities and knock out communications and take over, maybe shoot a few kids, and the Movement guerillas will go into the bush and start blowing up the water pipelines the Yanks will be building in places like this, to get the water down there."

He seemed very positive about it, as if it had happened already. I thought about the survival manuals: if the Movement guerillas were anything like David and Joe they would never make it through the winters. They couldn't get help from the cities, they would be too far, and the people there would be apathetic, they wouldn't mind another change of flag. If they tried at the outlying farms the farmers would take after them with shotguns. The Americans wouldn't even have to defoliate the trees, the guerillas would die of starvation and exposure anyway.

"Where will you get food?" I said.

"What do you mean 'you'?" he said. "I'm just speculating."

(96–97)

Yet while Atwood appears to ridicule the more extreme and more melodramatic manifestations of Canadian nationalism, there seems no doubt that she does this in order to salvage a realistic view of Canada's situation; she achieves this largely by stressing in *Surfacing*, even when she portrays a demonstrative nationalist like David, the extent to which Canada and Canadians have been Americanized. The difficulties of a small country with a powerful and persuasive neighbour she already stressed in *Survival*, when she suggested how shallow were the triumphs of the past on which the nationalists prided themselves.

The two historical moments at which mild congratulations might seem in order — the war of 1812 and the building of the trans-Canada railroad (or, for that, substitute Confederation; both symbolize the unifying of the country) — cannot sustain elation in the face of the irony of history: Canada repels invasion in 1812 and the Yanks take over anyway; Macdonald pulls the country together and now it's about to fall apart. (*Survival* 170)

It is the complicity of the Canadians in what is happening to them that Atwood emphasizes in both *Surfacing* and other writings, their willingness to be absorbed into the worldwide materialist consumer society that for her is represented by the Americans, whom she evidently blames for first creating that society's false values. She states her position very clearly in an essay called "Travels Back," which she published in *Maclean's* in 1973, the year after *Surfacing* appeared.

I don't think Canada is "better" than any other place, any more than I think Canadian literature is "better"; I live in one and read the other for a simple reason: they are mine, with all the sense of territory that implies. Refusing to acknowledge where you come from — and that must include the noodle man and his hostilities, the anti-nationalist lady and her doubts — is an act of amputation: you may become free floating, a citizen of the world (and in what other country is that an ambition?) but only at the cost of arms, legs or heart. By discovering your place you discover yourself.

But there's another image, fact, coming from the outside that I have to fit in. This territory, this thing that I have called "mine," may not be mine much longer. Part of the much-sought Canadian identity is that few nationals have done a more enthusiastic job of selling their country than have Canadians. Of course, there are buyers willing to exploit, as they say, our resources; there always are. It is our eagerness to sell that needs attention. Exploiting resources and developing potential are two different things: one is done from without by money, the other from within, by something I hesitate only for a moment to call love. (*Second Words* 113)

It is at this point that Atwood's various thematic preoccupations seem to converge. She sees the whole earth threatened by the urge to exploit its resources rather than to cultivate its potentialities with ecological awareness. Because she is Canadian and this is her part of the world, to which she is attached by all the mingled impulses that make up patriotism, she specifically defends Canada and its culture. In identifying its enemies as the "Americans" she is not attacking Americans as individuals; she is attacking the attitude first developed by American corporations, that the world is to be exploited freely for the benefit of the consumer society, no matter what its effect on ecological balances, no matter what its effect on the future of humanity. The narrator and her companions, aware though they are in a superficial, modish way of the American menace seen through the eyes of crude nationalism, are still trapped in the clichés of Americanized living.

At one point in *Survival*, Atwood remarks that "Poets incline towards Nature-as-woman metaphors; prose writers turn the metaphor around and use Woman-as-Nature" (202). And we can see in *Surfacing* the predicament of the landscape reflecting the narrator's predicament; both of them are the victims of assaults on the principle of life, for in terms of the novel one can regard the desolation of a valley to enlarge a lake as the analogue of the abortion of an embryo human being.†

Thus the situation of women in modern society is intimately connected with the issues of colonialism and of environmental exploitation. Atwood has said in *Second Words* (1982):

> I have always seen Canadian nationalism ... as part of a larger, non-exclusive picture. We sometimes forget, in our obsession with colonialism and imperialism, that Canada itself has been guilty of these stances towards others, both inside the country and outside it; and our concern about sexism, man's mistreatment of women, can blind us to the fact that men can be just as disgusting, and statistically more so, towards other men, and that women as members of certain national groups, although relatively powerless members, are not exempt from the temptation to profit at the expense of others. (282)

There are, I know, perils in assuming that Atwood held at the beginning of the 1970s, when she was writing *Surfacing*, the same views as she expressed in 1982, a decade later, yet there is no doubt that early on she began to resist attempts by critics to label her a feminist writer, and attempts by militant feminists to capture her for their movement. On this matter I think we can take an essay she wrote in 1976 for an anthology on the subject of the woman as writer

---

† Here I am making no judgement of how the clearly negative role of the abortion in *Surfacing* reflected Atwood's personal position in the abortion controversy. She has remained interestingly uncommunicative on this issue, and of course it would be unfair to judge her personal attitude on the basis of the obsessions of one of the characters.

as delineating the stand she held fairly consistently from the time she began to write novels.

> Some of my reservations have to do with the questionable value of writers, male or female, becoming directly involved in political movements of any sort: their involvement may be good for the movement, yet it has to be demonstrated that it's good for the writer. The rest concern my sense of the enormous complexity not only of the relationships between Man and Woman, but also of those between those other abstract intangibles, Art and Life, Form and Content, Writer and Critic, et cetera. (*Second Words* 190)

Of the early 1970s she remarked, at the same time, giving an implicit warning regarding the more extreme forms of feminism:

> This was also a period in which I was asked to review a number of books by women, and to speak and write about the same subject. I had of course reviewed books by women before . . . but "women" had now become a *subject*. I began to get worried about the possibility of a new ghetto: women's books reviewed only by women, men's books reviewed only by men, with a corresponding split in the readership. It wasn't what one had in mind as a desirable future for the species. (*Second Words* 106)

Yet since, as in all of Atwood's novels, the protagonist in *Surfacing* is female, we do have a novel written from the viewpoint of a female narrator, and according to that point of view women are dominated by men, and in some ways even more so when they are distanced from the accepted relationships of a traditional and more nature-oriented society. For example, though their roles are sharply differentiated, there is much more evident harmony between the old *canadien* farmer Paul and his wife than between those two pieces of modern urban flotsam, David and Anna. Yet David's weaselish brutality towards Anna, with its nagging meanness, speaks less of domination than of the insecurity of the male in a world where the old surenesses of role and status (bad as they were) have been lost and replaced by nothing better.

The narrator's attitude towards men goes through a significant metamorphosis. At first she feels guilt towards the imagined husband whom, in her false memory, she had deserted, leaving him with the child she never had. When she does recover her memory her guilt is transferred to the child she allowed to be aborted, and she feels a burning resentment towards the married lover who, as she sees it, morally forced her into this act and then, insult piled on injury, obliged her to go through the squalid backstreet operation on her own while he hosted a birthday party for his "legitimate" children. Yet at the end of the novel, when she has emerged from her trauma, she speaks of him with regretful understanding.

> I can remember him, fake husband, more clearly though, and now I feel nothing for him but sorrow. He was neither of the things I believed, he was only a normal man, middle-aged, second-rate, selfish and kind in the average proportions; but I am not prepared for the average, its needless cruelties and lies. (188–89)

With a sure artistry Atwood puts into the mouth of her narrator — at the time when her mental disturbance is reaching its height — the sentences that in their crazy way draw all the themes — sexual, political, and sociological — together. David has accused her of either hating men or wanting to be one, and she thinks without answering:

> Maybe it was true, I leafed through all the men I had known to see whether or not I had hated them. But then I realized it wasn't the men I hated, it was the Americans, the human beings, men and women both. They'd had their chance but they had turned against the gods, and it was time for me to choose sides. I wanted there to be a machine that could make them vanish, a button I could press that would evaporate them without disturbing anything else, that way there would be more room for the animals, they would be rescued. (154)

But there are no dramatic interventions. Nature stands, neutral and vulnerable. So far as it has a moral, *Surfacing* suggests that each person finds her own liberation, and individually seeks the liberation of her world, recognizing that myth is only the signature of reality, as the narrator eventually does.

In one of the earliest reviews of *Surfacing*, Christina Newman remarks that the novel "moves from the plain perceptions of the opening chapters on to the knife edge of madness and fantasy that are characteristic of Atwood's vision" (McCombs 43). Several critics have regarded the narrator as insane and *Surfacing* as a novel about madness. But the fact is that "I" 's experiences, as she transmits them to us, in fact form a process of shedding her crippling guilts and inhibitions and seeing the world anew as a liberated and integrated person.

Yet there are such speculations about the narrator's sanity that at times one begins to wonder whether it is not time to paraphrase Wilde's quip about *Hamlet* — are the critics of *Surfacing* mad or only pretending? For at times they become so clinically literal that they seem to be treating the book as if it were the case report on an actual person rather than the work of moral vision which it undoubtedly is. Yet such discussions have their value in guiding us to some of the possible sources of Atwood's strategy in projecting the mental state of her protagonist. One can even draw a certain wisdom from an extreme remark like Robert Kroetsch's that the "terror" of the narrator "lies not in her going insane but in her going sane" (McCombs 9). For in fact, as the very quality of her speech tells us, "I" is locked in protective and tightly controlled delusions at the beginning, and it is her dawning recognition of reality that plunges her into fear and crisis as the novel continues.

Surfacing actually appeared at a time when there was high interest in the theories of R.D. Laing, who opposed accepted psychiatric methods, taught that mental illness might well be a healthy response to a sick society, and that conventional authoritarian treatments might in fact hinder the self-directed resolution of personality disorders. To the extent that the narrator does resolve her problems without professional intervention, there seems some justification for those critics who stress Laing's influence, though in my view it was a matter of Atwood's absorbing and using ideas that happened to be current at the time rather than of attempting any deliberate explication of Laingian doctrine.

Other critics have found traces, and sometimes more than traces, of earlier forms of depth psychology in the predicament and the eventual recovery of the narrator. Frank Davey devoted one of the few books on Margaret Atwood to what is to all intents and purposes a Freudian interpretation, and certainly there is a distinct Freudian echo in the part played by the father, and in that of the forgotten middle-aged lover whose role as a surrogate father seems to have forced his expulsion from memory as a partner in transferred incest as well as the father of the aborted child.

Yet others see the influence of Jungian psychology; the parents and the brother are viewed as projections of ancient archetypes, and the narrator is perceived as seeking wholeness through her understanding of these images drawn from her own past but also from the collective unconscious. Though I am certain that Atwood has already absorbed the essence of all these approaches before she came to write *Surfacing*, to me it is the Jungian affinity that seems most dominant. The Jamesian ghosts which she herself emphasizes and which are projections of forces within the haunted person, seem very close to the Jungian archetypes.

Perhaps the most significant revelation which the narrator herself makes to us lies in her sense of the division within her between mental activity and, on the other hand, feeling (in the emotional sense) and physical sensation. At one point, when she tells Anna about her problems with Joe because she has refused to marry him, Anna says, "You must feel awful."

> I didn't feel awful; I realized that I didn't feel much of anything, I hadn't for a long time. Perhaps I'd been like that all my life, just as some babies are born deaf or without a sense of touch; but if that was true I wouldn't have noticed the absence. At some point my neck must have closed over, pond freezing or a wound, shutting me into my head; since then everything had been glancing off me, it was like being in a vase, or the village where I could see them but not hear them because I couldn't understand what was being said. Bottles distort for the observer too: frogs in the jam jar stretched wide, to them watching I must have appeared grotesque. (105–06)

And a little later, paddling in the lake in a heavy wind, she tells:

> Paddle digging the lake, ears filled with moving air; breath and sweat, muscle hurt, my body at any rate was alive. (112–13)

Despite Atwood's half-playful assurances that *Surfacing* is to be read as a ghost story, I think most critics and readers see it as a *rite de passage* in the classic manner, as Margaret Laurence does when, recalling to us "*The Golden Bough, Beowulf* or, somewhat more recently, Amos Tutuola's *The Palmwine Drunkard*," she continues:

> For it is the ancient Quest which is the journey here, the descent into the dark regions, where some special knowledge is gained, some revelation, before the return to the world of known creatures. The woman does return, and will go back to the world of humans, but she has been given a knowledge of her own power, a power which had frightened her and which she had therefore denied, and a knowledge of her previous willingness to be a victim, a willingness which had of course also victimized others. She has also, I think, been given another knowledge — the ancient gods of forest and lake are by no means dead; they are there, and attention must be paid. (McCombs 47)

The quest which is also the *rite de passage* by which a person discovers his or her own true inner self is not merely a matter of western literature or folklore. Lodged doubtless in the archetypal continuum which Jung called the Collective Unconscious, the quest finds its place not only in the great epic myths like the *Odyssey* and the tale of the Argonauts in the mediaeval knightly romances (of which *Don Quixote* was the grand parodic culmination), but also in the vast variety of initiation processes that are to be found among so-called primitive peoples of all races and languages. Such tales and such ceremonies emerge as it were spontaneously among peoples who can have had no connections with each other in past and present. One can find analogues for them in the stages of development through which most people pass in their lives, or, in the case of those who are mentally disturbed like the narrator, the stages by which such people can travel the journey that will bring them back to their true selves.

The resemblance between the narrator's experience in *Surfacing* and the rites of North American Indians has often been observed. Some critics (including me at one period) have cited the shamanic initiations which are shared by Siberian as well as North American aborigenes as an example, and Rosemary Sullivan has named Mircea Eliade's *Shamanism* as a possible source for *Surfacing*. But there are aspects of the shamanic rites, as recorded by Eliade and observed by ethnologists in British Columbia and among the Inuit, that do not find a place in the experiences of the narrator of *Surfacing*. In shamanic cults, the novice first goes through a period of association with an initiated shaman, and then, when he seems prepared, he sets out on a course of acute deprivation until, on the verge of death, he goes into a state of trance and experiences a series of delusions that varies surprisingly little from case to case. In this state he is transported magically to a haunt of the spirits of dead shamans, who perform certain rituals, including the symbolic dismemberment of his body and its reassembly in a kind of spiritual as well as physical rebirth. He emerges from the trance not only personally transformed, but also endowed with the magical powers that make the shaman the valued healer of his community, yet leave in him the possibility of becoming a dreaded sorcerer.

It is here that the analogy between what happens in *Surfacing* and the rituals of shamanic initiation break down, for in the last resort it is not a novel about magic but about self-realization. The narrator is not subjected to any transformation by magicians dead and gone; she does not emerge conscious of the possession of magical powers over other people, either for good or evil, though she is aware of a power within herself, and of her need to exert it.

> This above all, to refuse to be a victim. Unless I can do that I can do nothing. I have to recant, give up the old belief that I am powerless and because of it nothing I can do will ever hurt anyone. (191)

What Atwood describes is in fact much nearer to the spirit quests which Indians of many tribes, even if they are not aspiring shamans, will undertake. Among the Salish, for example, a man or a woman's future life may well be shaped by the spirit quest he or she undertakes. The novice becomes attached to a dance society and after undergoing certain ordeals imposed by its initiates, will go out into the wilderness to seek his guardian spirit. He observes certain taboos, goes naked in all weathers, deprives himself of food and drink, sleeps little and then rough, and eventually goes into the trance in which the spirit appears before him, either some mythical being or the supernatural manifestation of an animal. The spirit will teach the novice the dance and the song that will validate his name and be his exclusive possessions for the rest of his life. Moreover, the nature of the spirit is likely to determine the novice's future vocation. To meet the woodpecker spirit means a future as a woodcarver; the wolf stands for hunting and the hornet for the warrior's calling; the owl gives clairvoyance and the mythical snake predisposes the novice to shamanism.

Even with the Indian spirit quest the experience of the narrator is not precisely identical. When her companions are about to depart, she gets into a canoe and paddles away, concealing herself in the "landlocked swamp" of a bay on the island formed among tree stumps when the dam raised the water. She already senses her identity with the life around her.

> Through the trees the sun glances; the swamp around me smoulders, energy of decay turning to growth, green fire. I remember the heron; by now it will be insects, frogs, fish, other herons. My body also changes, the creature in me, plant-animal, sends out filaments in me; I ferry it secure between death and life, I multiply. (168)

And then she creeps through the vegetation to watch her companions depart.

> I walk to the hill and scan the shoreline, finding the place, opening, where they disappeared; checking, reassuring. It's true, I am by myself; this is what I wanted, to stay here alone. From any rational point of view I am absurd; but there are no longer any rational points of view. (169)

Solitude is, of course, a necessary condition of the spirit quest, and so is the shedding of all the attributes of human existence, of all that makes one human and social. She smashes everything that is breakable on the house, defaces the books, slashes the blankets and beds and eventually her own clothes to make them unusable. She burns all her drawings, past and present, and, most important to her, she burns all the images connected with her parents.

> Theirs too, the map torn from the wall, the rock paintings, left to me by my father's will; and the album, the sequence of my

mother's life, the confining photographs. . . . It is time that separates us, I was a coward, I would not let them into my age, my place. Now I must enter theirs. (177)

In other words, she must confront the guardian spirits, whether they be benign or fearful. And now she begins, like a spirit quester, to establish taboos that keep her away from anything planned and human. She must not enter the garden or the house, for the spirits shun them, like the Indian spirits which are to be met only in the wilderness.

They can't be anywhere that's marked out, enclosed: even if I opened the doors and fences they could not pass in to houses and cages, they can move only in the spaces between them, they are against borders. To talk with them I must approach the condition they themselves have entered; in spite of my hunger I must resist the fence, I'm too close now to turn back. (180)

And then, entranced by weakness, she sees her mother, feeding the jays as she always did.

I've stopped walking. At first I feel nothing except a lack of surprise: that is where she would be, she has been standing there all along. Then as I watch and it doesn't change I'm afraid, I'm cold with fear, I'm afraid it isn't real, paper doll cut by my eyes, burnt picture, if I blink she will vanish.

She must have sensed it, my fear. She turns her head quietly and looks at me, past me, as though she knows something is there but she can't quite see it. The jays cry again, they fly up from her, the shadows of their wings ripple over the ground and she's gone.

I go up to where she was. The jays are there in the trees, cawing at me; there are a few scraps in the feeding tray still, they've knocked some to the ground. I squint up at them, trying to see her, trying to see which one she is; they hop, twitch their feathers, turn their heads, fixing me first with one eye, then the other. (182)

A little later it is the spirit father, or rather his animal surrogate, that she sees. She goes to the garden and observes a figure there staring into it.

66

I say Father.

He turns towards me and it's not my father. It is what my father saw, the thing you meet when you've stayed here too long alone.

I'm not frightened, it's too dangerous for me to be frightened of it; it gazes at me for a time with its yellow eyes, wolf's eyes, depthless but lambent as the eyes of animals seen at night in the car headlights. Reflectors. It does not approve of me or disapprove of me, it tells me it has nothing to tell me, only the fact of itself.

Then its head swings away with an awkward, almost crippled motion: I do not interest it, I am part of the landscape, I could be anything, a tree, a deer skeleton, a rock. (186–87)

The wolf-being turns into a fish jumping in the lake, the "idea of a fish . . . antlered fish thing drawn in red on cliffstone, protecting spirit" (187). It hangs there above the water for what seems "an hour or so," and then drops and, as the circles of its falling widen, becomes a fish again.

The haunting has ended. Talking of *Surfacing* in an interview, Atwood once evoked "ghost lore" (presumably European) by which the ghost was not aware of its perceiver. In the case of the narrator's spirit they do not address her, they may not even see her, yet they seem aware of her, and the next day, after she has dreamt of their departure, she says "they spoke to me, in the other language" (188).

I once had the good fortune to be present at a Salish spirit dance, the annual occasion when the novices, returned from their quests, danced their personal dances, sang their personal songs, and were accepted as initiates. I was sitting next to some visiting Indians from another Salish band speaking the same dialect as our hosts. When an orator stood up at one point and I asked what he said, they claimed not to understand him. "It is another language," they said. "It is an old language the spirits speak."

The parallel between Salish spirit quests and the narrator's *rite de passage* seems even more evident when she remarks: "I saw them and they spoke to me, in the other language." They may not have given her a dance or a song, but they have given her the name she lacked through the novel and which Joe eventually speaks. They may not have given her a specific vocation, but they have given her a purpose

67

("To prefer life, I owe them that.") and a specific task, to fight against "the pervasive menace, the Americans."

> They exist, they're advancing, they must be dealt with, but possibly they can be watched and predicted and stopped without being copied. (189)

And so, as the narrator's *rite de passage* ends and she seems posed for re-entry into the world of cities and civilization, we know that she has come not merely to an understanding with herself. She has come also to an understanding, as the Initiates of Indian spirit dances are held to do, that the world of natural life and even inanimate entities like stones and storms must be respected since they are instinct with spirit.

One way of dividing writers is between those who are concerned with the journey, and whose interest is mainly in the making of the book, the form and the style; and those who are most concerned with the destination, the final statement that emerges from each work, novel or poem, story or play. Atwood as a novelist inclines towards being the destination writer, though the impeccable lapidary craftsmanship, the sure care with words and images that her prose shares with her verse, makes her also a journey writer. Destination for her is not really contained in the plot and its resolution, but rather in the often unspoken message which that resolution projects. She is, after all, a writer committed to the society in which she lives and to offering a true account of it, and inevitably she is concerned, in however general a way, with posing an alternative way of perceiving which might lead to an alternative way of doing. Human beings, she is saying, may be forced into living and perceiving in false, unnatural ways, but the harm that is done is not irremediable, the lie is not irreversible.

But the lie and the truth are not confined to the individual and his relationship with the world in which he finds himself; it applies to whole societies. They too have to make their choices between life and death, and behind the vision of an individual mind gone wrong which the narrator of *Surfacing* has to offer us, there is the much larger vision of a whole society gone wrong because of its misunderstanding of man's role within the ecological order. In the end, more than the colonization of Canada, more than the predicament of women, the matter of the environment is the great theme of *Surfacing*. For our attitudes towards each other as humans are seen as depending in the long run on our attitude towards other beings in the natural world and towards the earth itself. When we have abandoned the role of dominators and destroyers and recognized our place in the pattern, then we shall release ourselves from the perils that threaten us individually and our world in general. In this sense *Surfacing* offers a way back for us all.

Works Cited

Atwood, Margaret. *Bodily Harm*. Toronto: McClelland, 1981.

———. *The Circle Game*. Toronto: Contact, 1966.

———. *Double Persephone*. Toronto: Hawkshead, 1961.

———. *The Edible Woman*. 1969. New Canadian Library 93. Toronto: McClelland, 1973.

———. *The Journals of Susanna Moodie*. Toronto: Oxford UP, 1970.

———. *Power Politics*. Toronto: Anansi, 1971.

———. *Procedures for Underground*. Toronto: Oxford UP, 1970.

———. *Second Words: Selected Critical Prose*. Toronto: Anansi, 1982.

———. *Surfacing*. Toronto: McClelland, 1972.

———. *Survival: A Thematic Guide to Canadian Literature*. Toronto: Anansi, 1972.

———. "Writing the Male Character." *Second Words: Selected Critical Prose*. Toronto: Anansi, 1982. 412–30.

Broege, Valerie. "Margaret Atwood's Canadians and Americans." *Essays on Canadian Writing* 22 (1981): 111–35.

Brown, Russell M. "Atwood's Sacred Wells." *Essays on Canadian Writing* 17 (1980): 5–43.

Campbell, Josie P. "The Woman as Hero in Margaret Atwood's *Surfacing*." *Mosaic* 11.3 (1978): 17–28.

Campbell describes *Surfacing* as "a sort of psychological thriller, where the protagonist searches for or comes in conflict with that fragmented self which appears as a ghost," and makes a comparison with *Hamlet*. She also claims that *Surfacing* has been influenced by the works of Joseph Campbell.

Carrington, Ildikó de Papp. "Margaret Atwood and Her Works." *Canadian Writers and Their Works*. Fiction Series. Vol. 9. Ed. Robert Lecker, Jack David, and Ellen Quigley. Toronto: ECW, 1987. 25–116.

A detailed discussion of Atwood's life and works.

Christ, Carol P. "Margaret Atwood: The Surfacing of Woman's Spiritual Quest and Vision." *Signs: Journal of Women in Culture and Society* 2.2 (1976): 316–30.

Sees *Surfacing* as a feminist theological tract.

Cluett, Robert. "Surface Structures: The Syntactic Profile of *Surfacing*."

Margaret Atwood: Language, Text, and System. Ed. Sherrill Grace and Lorraine Weir. Vancouver: U of British Columbia P, 1983. 67–90.

Davey, Frank. "Margaret Atwood." *From There to Here: A Guide to English-Canadian Literature since 1960.* Our Nature — Our Voices, Vol. II. Erin, ON: Porcépic, 1974. 30–36.

A brief survey of Atwood's work.

_____. *Margaret Atwood: A Feminist Poetics.* Vancouver: Talonbooks, 1984.

Davidson, Arnold E., and Cathy N. Davidson, eds. *The Art of Margaret Atwood: Essays in Criticism.* Toronto: Anansi, 1981.

Garebian, Keith. " 'Surfacing': Apocalyptic Ghost Story." *Mosaic* 9.3 (1976): 1–9.

Garebian examines the structure of the novel, its major themes, and Atwood's postulates about the heroine and her ghosts which "are essentially projections of the protagonist's troubled mind."

Gibson, Graeme. "Margaret Atwood." *Eleven Canadian Novelists.* Toronto: Anansi, 1973. 1–31.

An interview which includes detailed discussion of *Surfacing.*

Grace, Sherrill. *Violent Duality: A Study of Margaret Atwood.* Montreal: Véhicule, 1980.

_____, and Lorraine Weir, eds. *Margaret Atwood: Language, Text, and System.* Vancouver: U of British Columbia P, 1983.

Guédon, Marie Francoise. "Surfacing: Amerindian Themes and Shamanism." *Margaret Atwood: Language, Text, and System.* Ed. Sherrill Grace and Lorraine Weir. Vancouver: U of British Columbia P, 1983. 91–111.

Horne, Alan J. "Margaret Atwood: An Annotated Bibliography (Prose)." *The Annotated Bibliography of Canada's Major Authors.* Ed. Robert Lecker and Jack David. Vol. I. Downsview, ON: ECW, 1979. 13–46.

Hutcheon, Linda. "From Poetic to Narrative Structure: The Novels of Margaret Atwood." *Margaret Atwood: Language, Text, and System.* Ed. Sherrill Grace and Lorraine Weir. Vancouver: U of British Columbia P, 1983. 17–31.

James, William C. "Atwoods's Surfacing." *Canadian Literature* 91 (1981): 174–81.

Keith, W.J. *Canadian Literature in English.* Longman Literature in English Series. London: Longman, 1985.

Larkin, Joan. "Soul Survivor." *Ms.* May 1973: 33–34.

A positive review of *Surfacing* that insists that the book should not be read as the story of the alienated young; rather it is about rebirth and return.

Lecker, Robert. "Janus through the Looking Glass: Atwood's First Three Novels." *The Art of Margaret Atwood: Essays in Criticism.* Ed. Arnold E. Davidson and Cathy N. Davidson. Toronto: Anansi, 1981. 177–203.

McCombs, Judith, ed. *Critical Essays on Margaret Atwood.* Boston: Hall, 1988.

Mendez-Egle, Beatrice, and James M. Haule, eds. *Margaret Atwood: Reflection and Reality.* Edinburg, TX: Pan American U, 1987.

Miner, Valerie. "Atwood in Metamorphosis: An Authentic Canadian Fairy Tale." *Her Own Woman: Profiles of Ten Canadian Women.* Ed. Myrna Kostash. Toronto: Macmillan, 1975. 173–94.

A useful interview in the biographical details it provides of Atwood's childhood and the influence of her parents.

Moss, John. *A Reader's Guide to the Canadian Novel.* Toronto: McClelland, 1981.

New, W.H. "Fiction." *Literary History of Canada: Canadian Literature in English.* 2nd ed. 3 vols. Ed. Carl F. Klinck. Toronto: U of Toronto P, 1976. 3: 273–74.

Newman, Christina. "In Search of a Native Tongue." *Maclean's* Sept. 1972: 88.

Newman sees *Surfacing* as being important in several ways, particularly in its description of what goes on in the mind of a woman trying to deal with the brutalities and pressures imposed by the politics of sex.

Northey, Margot. "Sociological Gothic: 'Wild Geese' and 'Surfacing.' " *The Haunted Wilderness: The Gothic and Grotesque in Canadian Fiction.* Toronto: U of Toronto P, 1976. 62–69.

Surfacing is an example of "sociological gothic" as it contains elements belonging to the fantastic world of romance and to realistic or analytic fiction.

Ondaatje, Michael. Rev of *The Circle Game. Canadian Forum* April 1967: 22–23.

Onley, Gloria. "Margaret Atwood: Surfacing in the Interests of Survival." *West Coast Review* 7.3 (1973): 51–54.

Sees Atwood's work as being significant because it is "so clearly in tune with the radical spirit of her times."

Piercy, Marge. "Margaret Atwood: Beyond Victimhood." *American Poetry Review* 2.6 (1973): 41–44.

Pratt, Annis. "*Surfacing* and the Rebirth Journey." *The Art of Margaret Atwood: Essays in Criticism.* Ed. Arnold E. Davidson and Cathy N. Davidson. Toronto: Anansi, 1981. 139–57.

Rigney, Barbara Hill. *Margaret Atwood.* London: Macmillan Education, 1987.

Rosenberg, Jerome H. *Margaret Atwood.* Boston: Twayne, 1984.

_____ . "Woman as Everyman in Atwood's 'Surfacing': Some Observations on the End of the Novel." *Studies in Canadian Literature* 3.1 (1978): 127–32.

Attempts to describe Atwood's literary and sociological intention in *Surfacing.*

Rubinstein, Roberta. "Escape Artists and Split Personalities: Margaret Atwood." *Boundaries of the Self: Gender, Culture, Fiction.* Urbana: U of Illinois P, 1987. 63–122.

Rule, Jane. "Life, Liberty, and the Pursuit of Normalcy: The Novels of Margaret Atwood." *Malahat Review* 41 (1977): 42–49.

Discusses the pursuit of normalcy by characters in *The Edible Woman, Surfacing,* and *Lady Oracle.* To the narrator in *Surfacing,* normalcy is terrifying and important.

Sandler, Linda. "Interview with Margaret Atwood." *Malahat Review* 41 (1977): 5–27.

Schaeffer, Susan Fromberg. " 'It is Time that Separates Us': Margaret Atwood's *Surfacing.*" *Centennial Review* 18.4 (1974): 319–37.

Schaeffer believes that *Surfacing* is about mortality and the victimization of all mankind, and is wrongly interpreted as being about the victimization of women.

Skelton, Robin. Rev. of *The Journals of Susanna Moodie*. *Malahat Review* 17 (1971): 133–34.

Sullivan, Rosemary. "Margaret Atwood." *Oxford Companion to Canadian Literature*. Ed. William Toye. Toronto: Oxford UP, 1983. 30–33.

_____. "Surfacing and Deliverance." *Canadian Literature* 67 (1976): 6–20.

Sullivan contrasts *Surfacing* to James Dickey's *Deliverance* in order to identify what is peculiarly Canadian about Atwood's novel.

VanSpanckeren, Kathryn, and Jan Garden Castro, eds. *Margaret Atwood: Vision and Forms*. Carbondale: Southern Illinois UP, 1988.

Woodcock, George. "Margaret Atwood." *Contemporary Novelists*. Ed. D.L. Kirkpatrick. New York: St. Martin's, 1986. 48–51.

_____. "Margaret Atwood: Poet as Novelist." *The World of Canadian Writing: Critiques & Recollections*. Vancouver: Douglas, 1980. 149–73.

_____. "Surfacing to Survive: Notes of the Recent Atwood." *Ariel* 4.3 (1973): 16–28.

Surfacing is a novel of self-realization, but it also possesses an element of self-criticism. At the end of the novel there is sanity, a real understanding of reality.

Updated checklists of Atwood scholarship are now published annually in the *Newsletter of the Margaret Atwood Society* (ed. Jerome Rosenberg, Dept. of English, Miami University, Akron, Ohio).

Index